A Companion Guide

to

The River Quintet Series

YOUNG LIVES IN A CHANGING WORLD

A Companion Guide to The River Quintet Series

YOUNG LIVES IN A CHANGING WORLD

Joan G. Sheeran

Quill Publications | USA

QuillPublications.com

Copyright © 2024 Quill Publications

ISBN: 979-8-9899063-0-7

Typesetting by C'est Beau Designs

Contents

PART I

Introduction

A.

The River Quintet Series:
Young Lives in a Changing World

The title refers to a series of historical novels written by Ray E. Phillips, M.D. The series is comprised of five integrated yet "stand alone" books set in the 17th century. The lives of members of an Iroquois-Mohawk family are vividly portrayed, along with those of a Dutch boy and an English girl. The characters range in age from (approximately) 13 to 18. Each book offers a realistic picture of the challenges and social makeup of the time as experienced by the main characters. Each one is accompanied by additional information to enhance the reader's understanding and appreciation of places and concepts.

Books 1, 2, 3, and 5 contain **Reference Notes** on a variety of subjects that include life in a Mohawk village in the woodlands of northeastern North America, on a ship from Holland making an oceanic voyage, at a Dutch trading post on the Hudson River, and in a manor house in England. Specifics include the Iroquois longhouse, animals, plants, geological formations, historical events, and physical ailments. Since these Notes or "mini essays" are placed at the end of each book, they do not interfere with page-by-page reading. <u>Book 4 has no Notes.</u> Because it is narrated in the "first person singular," that is, in diary form, it is followed by another kind of reference format: a **Historical Framework** consisting of an *Overview of events in 17th century Europe,* as these events relate to the main character, and a *Timeline* **1613-1692** of relevant historical facts. The various types of reference material in the individual books add to the overall value and uniqueness of the series.

 Age groups/grade levels: Appealing perhaps most to the young adult reader, the series focuses on characters who struggle with the age-old problems of growing up. Their experiences are far-ranging. Some characters carry heavier physical and psychological burdens than others, and these become integral features of their own personal challenges. As the series progresses, issues of social justice, belief systems and morality are raised; as a result, the life-stories of the main characters become increasingly more complex. Books 1 and 2, therefore, may be more suitable for students in grades 7 and 8, whereas Books 3, 4 and 5 may be appreciated better by older students who are more knowledgeable about world events: those in grades 9 through 12. Of course, there are always exceptions, and teachers should consider their students' abilities and individual needs.

 The title of the series also refers to specific bodies of water. In North America, the stories unfold along the Hudson River, called the *Co-ha-ta-ted-a* by the Mohawks and *Noordrivier* (North River) by the Dutch, the East River, and the Harlem River (actually, estuaries or tidal straits), and the Connecticut River, called *Versche Rivier* (Fresh River) by the Dutch. In England, the title refers to the River Thames and its tributary, the Ash. In the Dutch Republic there is the *Zuiderzee*, (Southern or South Sea), which in the 17th century was an inlet of the North Sea. These waterways, together with the Atlantic Ocean, establish a geographic framework that connects all the action in the five books.

The Five Books of the Series: Synopses

1. *Tail Feather: Adventures of a Mohawk Paddler on the River-That-Flows-Two-Ways*

2. *Laughing Rain and Awakens Corn: Look-the-Same Girls in the Land of the Cloud-Splitter*

3. *Johannes van der Zee: Journey of a Dutch Sailor to a Trading Post in New Netherland*

 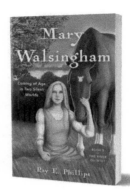

4. *Sky Flower: Memoirs of a Mohawk Woman at the Edge of Two Worlds*

5. *Mary Walsingham: Coming of Age in Two Silent Worlds*

Website link: https://quillpublications.com/the-river-quintet
Search: Ray E. Phillips-The River Quintet

Synopsis of Book 1

TAIL FEATHER: Adventures of a Mohawk Paddler on the River-That-Flows-Two-Ways

The arrival of a copper trader from the far-away land of the Great Waters makes a dramatic impression on a shy, adolescent Mohawk boy. Tail Feather, being left-handed and feeling different from all his friends, thinks he now has a chance to prove that he is capable of great challenges and adventures. Although his effort to catch up with the Running Man on his return trek fails, the boy finds another way to impress his peers: a lone trip up to the top of Cloud-Splitter (Mt. Marcy). This, too, ends in near disaster when he is almost captured by an enemy band of Hurons (Wendats). Hoping next to join his elders in their annual trading expedition, Tail Feather tries to impress everyone with his diligence and skill in performing tribal tasks. Finally, the elders agree that he may travel with them. Preparations involve canoe making and a steam ritual.

The downriver journey to the end of the River-That-Flows-Two-Ways (the Hudson River) provides Tail Feather with new vistas and experiences: cultural revelations about the Algonquin tribes residing along the river and geographical and natural features such as cascades, rocky cliffs, briny water, and marshlands. In addition, the trip will expose him to frightening and dangerous situations: a passage through enemy (Mohican) territory and a near escape from hostile warriors in war canoes. Illness and physical suffering are part of the long journey, too. Unexpected even by Tail Feather's older traveling companions is the sight of a Dutch sailing ship, that of Adriaen Block. Whereas the older Mohawks cannot understand this phenomenon and its meaning, Tail Feather is curious about it.

At their destination, the island where the trading of flint for shells and other items takes place, Tail Feather finally sees the ocean and the "monster" described by elders in the Night Stories. His father assures him that he has never needed to prove himself worthy of respect: all he had to do was to believe in himself.

Synopsis of Book 2

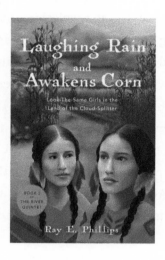

LAUGHING RAIN AND AWAKENS CORN:
Look-the-Same Girls in the Land of the Cloud-Splitter

With mixed emotions Laughing Rain and Awakens Corn watch their brother, Tail Feather, paddle away on the biggest adventure yet of his life. The girls are proud that he was chosen to take part in the important annual trading expedition. They are also sad because they will miss him. Awakens Corn is overcome by another emotion: the desire to have, someday, a great adventure of her own. She shocks her sister with this revelation because the Mohawk way of life has a strict code regarding gender roles and expectations of men and women.

Arguments and hurt feelings begin to challenge the once warm and special relationship the identical twins shared until now. Awakens Corn understands that women's domestic duties are vital to the well-being of the community, just as the men's are, but still, she would like a chance to do something big and different at least once in her life. Why can she not travel outside the clan? A compromise, of sorts, is provided when their mother allows them to take a day for their pleasure: a walk around the lake. On this excursion they confront a French missionary whom they take to their village. Few people understand what he tries to tell them, and most are unwilling to exchange their beliefs for a stranger's strange words. Awakens Corn is curious, nonetheless.

After more arguments with her sister, she runs away, climbing up Cloud-Splitter to seek solace and the reason she cannot be content. Lost and injured, she is rescued by her brother's wolf, Kykoo, who leads her home. Instead of scolding her for running away, Chief Red Sun tells both girls about his own childhood adventure as a runaway Abenaki, and how he was raised by Mohawks. He also reminds them about Peacemaker Hiawatha. The girls must learn to accept their different viewpoints and co-exist peacefully. There will be no punishment for Awakens Corn. Another compromise is made. Laughing Rain accepts her sister's offer to show her the pond on top of Cloud-Splitter.

Synopsis of Book 3

JOHANNES VAN DER ZEE: Journey of a Dutch Sailor to a Trading Post in New Netherland

Once a cabin boy on Adriaen Block's ship *Tijger* in 1613, Johannes is now—three years later—a seaman sailing again to New Netherland. His enthusiasm fades when he witnesses the cruel punishments of the sailors and the dangers and severe hardships on this oceanic voyage. When he nearly falls off a mast, a Danish sailor reaches out to save him. Ingmar tells him about voyages in Arctic waters and escapades with pirates. Johannes befriends Reginald, the new cabin boy who will die trying to obey an order. Because his father is a wealthy merchant, and an investor in this expedition, Johannes is invited by the captain into his quarters for a brief exchange. He also learns about navigational instruments.

The arrival at the trading post is not joyful. European goods are exchanged for beaver pelts. All but one of the traders are replaced by those just arriving, including Johannes. During the ensuing winter months, the young sailor escapes from his quarrelsome mates by finding wood to chop. He comes upon the same *Wilde* whom he had seen while on the *Tijger*. Their friendship with sign language is met with distrust and rage by the Dutch crew members. One shoots a Mohican trader who had come to the post with pelts. With the trading mission now greatly jeopardized, Joost, the leader, allows Tail Feather to accompany his new friend to Tahawus. He hopes that the Mohawks might be willing to supply more of the needed beaver pelts.

In the mountain village Johannes sees a community of people busy at the tasks of survival: the making of canoes, clothing, and other provisions. He discovers that Native people are not ignorant of civilized behavior: they are both clever and conscientious and have values and culture. His attraction to Awakens Corn, however, is not appreciated, and he and Tail Feather return to the trading post – only to see it submerging during a spring flood. After an episode of poison ivy and other misadventures he is ready to return to Holland with new understandings of himself and the people in the "New World." With Tail Feather's help the young sailor will get to New Amsterdam and find a ship for his voyage home.

Synopsis of Book 4

SKY FLOWER: Memoirs of a Mohawk Woman at the Edge of Two Worlds

Introducing the story of *Sky Flower* is a preface describing the discovery of her memoirs and the lengthy process by their current owners to find a publisher. The memoirs begin as diary entries in the year 1692 when Sky Flower starts to relay events of the past as well as the present. Using a black quill, the legacy of an injured crow, she writes that she was once (because of her sun-sensitive skin) spoiled by her sisters. Villagers considered her lazy. She describes the first encounters of her people with European missionaries and traders, her stay in a primitive Dutch village (Fort Orange) caring for a sick girl, and finally, her severe disfigurement by smallpox. This devastating event forces Sky Flower to rethink her life's goals and to develop her inner resources. Her new knowledge of Dutch, reading, and arithmetic, gained by helping Katrina with her lessons, now serves her well. She gets passage on a ship headed downriver and cleverly points out errors in the ship's ledgers. With a letter of introduction by the grateful captain, Sky Flower finds lodging and employment as a maid at a tavern in *Nieuw Amsterdam*.

The tavern becomes her classroom: from observing and listening to sailors from around the world, Sky Flowers learns words in Portuguese, Norwegian, and English, and hears stories about far-away places. She also learns to deal swiftly with the unruly behavior of drunken sailors. She notes that the inhabitants of this village are of mixed races, not at all like the people of her clan.

A merchant at the tavern arranges a job for her in England. Sky Flower accepts a position in a well-to-do family in Littleton (now Shepperton). Once she discovers that deafness is the reason behind the youngest daughter's misbehavior, Sky Flower invents a plan to help Mary communicate. The two girls bond as they create hand-signals for common objects, actions, and feelings. She serves the children as governess for seven years, eagerly learning from their tutors. Over time she becomes disappointed by the expectations and double standards of English society. After a romantic misadventure she returns to New Netherland. Just north of Fort Orange and the new village of Beverwyck she starts a school for children of mixed heritage. In later years she renounces her "civilized" lifestyle, with its conflicting ethical values, and chooses to reside in a simple cabin built in the style of an Iroquois longhouse.

Synopsis of Book 5

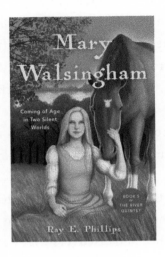

MARY WALSINGHAM: Coming of Age in Two Silent Worlds

As a child Mary had always proven to be misfit. Her parents, Lord and Lady Walsingham of Littleton, England, were perplexed. Her disruptive ways exasperated the entire household and left Mary bewildered, isolated, and unhappy. At the age of nine the cause of her trouble-making is discovered by the new child-minder, a young Native American woman named Sky Flower: Mary is deaf.

Mary and Sky Flower begin to develop their own language using hands and facial expressions. Mary proves to be intelligent, resourceful, and talented, particularly in drawing. She also has a winning way with animals. Still, she remains misunderstood by her family. Ever-deepening bonds between Mary and her governess are inevitable. After seven years, Sky Flower suddenly leaves the manor house for a romantic interest, leaving Mary crushed in spirit. Her recovery from this devastating blow comes from the opportunity of raising her own new-born foal. The two become totally devoted.

Determined to spare her horse from the traditional plow or fox chase, Mary, now at age sixteen, uses her ingenuity to accompany her horse to an English colony in the Americas. The ocean voyage is not easy, as she receives no help in caring for all the animals onboard. While staying with a Puritan family in the colony of Hartford, she witnesses religious customs quite different from those of her Anglican faith. Unwittingly, she finds herself helping others cope with their own personal challenges. Mary develops a special interest in Pieter, a young trader from New Netherland who has come to a Dutch fort nearby. The predictable romance, however, is not predictable. Mary's final task is to decide what she wants to do with her life: to go back to the Manor where—her father assures her—she could implement her own horse training methods, or to marry Pieter.

C.

Purpose of the Companion Guide

The general purpose of the *Guide* is to facilitate understanding of the series and to offer ideas for its use in a classroom setting.

This general purpose has three specific goals:

1. to point out the educational value of the series
2. to connect the series to curriculum goals, including historical insights and literary analyses
3. to suggest possibilities for assessments and opportunities for critical thinking, creative expression, and personal research

This book is an interdisciplinary teaching tool, serving as a starting point for classroom discussions of historical events and their depiction in literary works. Recognizable throughout the five novels are two humanitarian ideals long held by the author, Dr. Phillips: one, acceptance of people of other races, religions, and cultures, and of those challenged by physical and mental afflictions, and two, the recognition that love for humanity also means love for Planet

Earth and respect for all its creatures. Their goal: **the reduction of cultural prejudices that lead to social inequities and human conflict, and the advancement of mutual understanding and kindness.** These ideals will hopefully be evident in the commentaries, analyses, and assessment questions.

The varied topics presented throughout the series should be of interest not only to teachers of Social Studies but also to teachers of English, geography, health, and environmental science. Team Teaching of one or all the novels—either at the middle or high school level—may be a desirable approach for sharing and presenting lessons. Teachers may also like to create small student focus groups to discuss specific topics, such as the Iroquois longhouse or modes of travel in the 17th century.

Teachers of special needs students and parents engaged in homeschooling should modify the assessment and project suggestions to the educational needs or "Individual Educational Programs" of their students. A child with reading challenges may benefit occasionally from listening as another person reads aloud. Hands-on projects that include artwork or oral summaries of the plot are meaningful ways for students to demonstrate understanding of core elements in the novels. The home-school teachers of students of all abilities will know best how to inspire their own children to find the "moral of the story" and express that message in their own words.

GOAL 1: To Point Out the Educational Value of the River Quintet Series

General Pedagogical Benefits

As an addition to a school library or as classroom reading, each novel in The River Quintet series offers a story that is informative and inspiring. It is one that can become a catalyst for independent thinking in any number of areas. The merits are far-reaching:

1. The novels blend widely divergent historical events and settings, offering students glimpses into the social conditions in the 17th century: Native American settlements and those of early colonial America, the lifestyle of privileged classes in England, and the rigors of ocean travel.

2. Character development is a major element in each story. Examples involve acceptance of those who are "different": left-handed; seemingly uncultured; deaf and mute; scarred; and those considered odd or non-traditional according to cultural standards.

3. Each novel fosters self-confidence in the young protagonists.

4. Each novel addresses social attitudes regarding appropriate behavior for certain cultures.

5. Natural feelings are expressed in demanding situations: self-confidence and its lack, anticipation, fear, exhilaration, disappointment, heart-breaking loss, and affection.

6. Health issues are incorporated with some insight in how they were managed at this period of history. Illnesses such as smallpox, fevers, appendicitis, migraine headaches, and the "bloody flux" (dysentery) are described. The treatments reflect both the European medical practices of the 1600s and the methods used by Native Americans to deal with various afflictions.

GOAL 2: To Connect the Series to Curriculum Goals, Including Historical Insights and Literary Analyses

Goal 2 correlates with Part II: Understanding the Series

A. Compatibility of the Series with a Social Studies Curriculum

Remarks are based on the New York State Social Studies Framework, K-12.

B. Use of the Series in a Social Studies Curriculum

Historical, sociological, and psychological highlights—including how economic, geographical, and cultural factors affect various societies.

C. Use of the Series in an English Language Arts Curriculum

Topics regarding language in terms of age and grade level appropriateness; 17th century English spelling; vocabulary and literary aspects

D. Reference Section

Reproduced from the novels for easy access:

- Lists of Notes for Books 1, 2, 3, and 5
- Historical Framework for Book 4: Overview (17th Century and The Life of Sky Flower) and Global Timeline 1613-1692

GOAL 3: To Suggest Possibilities for Assessments and Opportunities for Critical Thinking, Creative Expression, and Personal Research

Goal 3 correlates with Part III: Assessment Suggestions
- Matching activity: identifying names of characters and places
- Pre-reading word lists
- Content questions for reading comprehension, with answers
- Questions for promoting critical thinking, personal reflection, and further discussion

Goal 3 correlates with Part IV: Projects and Class Activities
Suggestions for multisensory engagement with the novels, either individually or as a set; activities for students of all abilities

Goal 3 correlates with Part V: Resources for Further Study
Review Chart: Facts and Fiction. Timeline aligning fictional events with historical events. Readers will be able to put the fictional events into historical perspective.

Website Links and Suggested Reading. Resources for further information. See also: the Reference Section in Goal 2D above.

PART II

Understanding the Series

A.

Compatibility of the Series with Curriculum Goals

Although American state curriculum frameworks for history and social studies programs may vary, all would naturally include the beginnings of each state's history: the Native American presence in that state prior, during, and after the European incursion. In recent years many tribal nations have been taking an active role in helping states to update their curriculum standards. The general goal is to bring awareness of all students, whether Native or non-Native, to the history and culture of the various Indigenous groups that may populate their home states.

Since The River Quintet focuses on tribes in what is now New York State, it is appropriate to consult that state's educational *Framework*. Accordingly, the study of this topic in New York State spirals upward, starting in grade 4, intensifying in grades 7 and 8, and culminating in grades 9 and 10. Other state frameworks may vary the grade levels, but all presumably provide similar learning standards. Among these, as outlined in New York State's *Framework*[1] is the requirement that students

---

1 See: www.nysed.gov, New York State Social Studies Framework, K-12

learn to interpret historical facts and view events from more than one perspective. At advanced levels they should be able to analyze historical data, identify specific causes and effects of historical events, make cultural comparisons, and offer personal viewpoints. Ancillary sources such as literary works may serve to deepen their comprehension of a given topic or key idea.

The River Quintet offers five stories, each with unique perspectives regarding customs and prejudices of certain societies as observed by the title characters. **Native Americans:** Keeping tribal members strongly bound to their traditional cultures is sacred wisdom handed down by generations of elders and storytellers. Through the eyes of an Iroquois-Mohawk boy (Tail Feather in Book 1) the customs of scattered Algonquin groups are described. All five books portray various tribes to a greater or lesser degree. **The Dutch:** Representing Dutch society in New Netherland are two households, (a family in Fort Orange and a tavern owner and his wife in New Amsterdam), as well as a fort along the Connecticut River. Dutch ships, hauling away pelts, provide an economic slant to the colony. Foremost in this society is the value of commercial success. **The English:** Representing English society is a handful of diverse characters: clergymen, nobles, merchants, servants, sailors, traders, actors, religious outcasts, and the very poor. Their lives are conditioned by the power of the Church of England, ongoing religious conflicts, and an economic system dependent on menial labor. The manor house in Book 4, in fact, reflects these societal divisions. **Others:** Outside of this sphere, the reader senses, is the wild world of piracy where commercial greed and religious and political affiliations join in a toxic mix.

Finally, but not least important, is the **cast of major characters,** four Mohawk siblings, one Dutch boy and one English girl, whose lives are impacted by both cultural traditions as well as their own talents and aspirations. A reader may be inspired to reevaluate historical events based on the multiple experiences of these various characters in these various settings.

In Brief:

Focus on Indigenous North America, New Netherland, and England

The five books share the same geographical settings but in different degrees. Books 1, 2 and most of Book 3 describe the lifestyles of woodland tribes in 1613 and 1616. Book 4 provides a broad view of life in New Netherland and England from ca. 1628 to 1638, including an overview of relevant events until 1692. Book 5 brings together Native American, Dutch, and English societies about 1638-39 in New Netherland and in a Puritan-English colony along the Connecticut River.

Since the social studies curriculum in many states begins with the study of local Indigenous tribes, it is clear that the novels of The River Quintet series complement such a focus. In addition, the plots of the various stories involve sociological, ethical, and economic concerns caused by the admixture of the Dutch, English, and Native cultures. Understanding these issues is also a priority in a typical middle school curriculum.

Encouragement of Historical Objectivity

Readers might understand, through these five stories, how religious and legal institutions of mainstream societies (such as those of the English and the Dutch) can exert profound influence and power over the lives of all individuals in their jurisdictions, especially those cast into subservient roles. Readers might also begin to view historical events more objectively and less often through the distorting lens of personal prejudices. As in the example of the missionary in Book 2 or Johannes in Book 3: Would the reader recognize the morality and ingenuity of Native Americans or consider Indigenous peoples to be only *Wilden* (pronounced VIL-den), a term the Dutch used for those uncultured and in need of religious conversion? At the same time, readers should not undervalue the benefits of technology and the arts that "civilized" Europe of the time has introduced.

Readers of the series may interpret specific events positively or negatively, discover a new slant on a treatment of a familiar subject, and spot a connection between cultural traditions and personal prejudices. To offer their own opinions about historical events would be a natural extension.

Path to Good Citizenship

A long-term curriculum goal of the *Social Studies Framework* is good citizenship, that is, to prepare the student to engage productively in civic affairs. Contributing to the success of this goal is not only knowledge of one's national history and cultural heritage, but also of oneself: the knowledge of how to utilize one's talents in terms of career choices and community involvement, and how to interact with others of different customs and beliefs. As characters in the series demonstrate, a talented young person can become a contributing community member and a productive citizen.

B.

The Social Studies Curriculum

As a supplemental teaching tool, The River Quintet series offers **the middle and the high school reader** (and certainly anyone older) richly drawn portraits of the early stages of American history and a view of English life about the same time. The fictional timespan of the 17th century covers events in North America, England, and Holland, the latter being a lowlands province that would become part of the seven united provinces of the Dutch Republic. In this so-called Contact Period, the Native people of the northeastern woodlands encounter Dutch and French explorers; at the same time, English settlers reach far into New Netherland territory. Each of the five books gives the reader a different perspective of the constantly changing cultural landscape of the North American continent. Book 4, in addition, offers a view of English life as experienced by a Mohawk girl. To help the reader understand the background of the stories, there are reference notes in Books 1, 2, 3 and 5 and a historical overview and a global timeline in Book 4.

Features of The River Quintet Series

1. **the relationship of geography and the natural environ-
    ment to the economic and cultural well-being of a society.**
    Examples: a) copper carried by Native American runners from
    the upper Midwest and traded to Mohawks for flint, and flint,
    in turn, traded in coastal regions for seashells for use in sacred
    rites. b) the effect of coastal locations on Dutch and English
    maritime prosperity.

2. **the prominence of strong cultural traditions and
    religious or spiritual beliefs** in the lives of individuals, both
    Native American and European.

3. **the integration of single race societies (Native American,
    white, and Black) into multiracial and multicultural
    communities**. In this regard, Book 4 provides the most
    comprehensive view of such change: the village of New
    Amsterdam and England itself, despite rigid class structures.
    The international crews of all four ships are multicultural
    communities as well.

4. **the attention to matters of health.** The series shows that
    medical issues affect people in all time periods of human history.

*Overall, the series expands the reader's awareness of the geographical,
cultural, and economic dimensions of a given society. At the same time, it
presents stories of young people, who by trial and error, begin to recognize
their own talents and become determined to manage their own lives. **The
series encourages both self-confidence and independent thinking, two
values that would easily align with various state curriculum guidelines.***

Historical, Sociological and Psychological Aspects

The following observations highlight aspects of the series that should be relevant to a social studies curriculum dealing with the exploration and settlement of the North American continent. These remarks are by no means complete. In fact, they may generate more suggestions and classroom discussions. Teachers will want to add their own insights and interpretations.

In **Book 1,** *Tail Feather,* the reader learns about **tribal expectations** and how they affect a Mohawk boy in the year 1613. The reader also shares Tail Feather's joy as he is finally considered grown-up enough to travel with his elders on a momentous journey by canoe to the mouth of the River-That-Flows-Two-Ways (that is, the Hudson River), all the way to the Atlantic Ocean. Along the way the young paddler confronts other tribes, both hostile and friendly, who provide him with **new experiences**: a punishing game of war, the use of nets to catch fish, a frantic pursuit by a war canoe that is interrupted by a storm, healers applying their skills at driving away the evil spirit of sickness, brightly decorated traders busy at their commercial activities, and a ride in a dug-out canoe out into the ocean.

Before he reaches the ocean, however, Tail Feather has a different kind of experience. He confronts a strange object that resembles an enormous snow goose. It is a tall ship from Holland sailing upriver. People like no others he has ever seen before stare down at him as he sits awestruck in his birch canoe. This fictional event corresponds to the **historical event of Adriaen Block's voyage in 1613.**

The reader will discover that the **hazards of traveling** in this long-ago time had as much to do with physical pain and adverse weather conditions as with encounters of unfriendly tribes. Along Tail Feather's river journey the reader will realize that afflictions such as poison ivy and appendicitis as well as chills from hypothermia can happen to any human being regardless of the century in question. Understanding **the role of disease and physical ailments in historical narratives** helps today's reader see the human aspect of history. It also reinforces the notion that history can be viewed as series of human stories rather than merely a listing of factual events.

One of the major focal points in Book 1 is the psychological aspect of an **awkward adolescent** who, for various reasons, feels different from his peers and not taken seriously by the adults. Tail Feather's preference for the left hand also makes him stand out uncomfortably from others his age. His mistakes and his successes are noteworthy in a "coming of age" story.

Book 2, *Laughing Rain and Awakens Corn,* concerns the **societal and cultural changes** that are slowly and irrevocably taking place in both the Iroquois settlements upriver and the Algonquin areas downriver. The Mohawk girls after whom Book 2 is named are Tail Feather's identical twin sisters in their early adolescent years. The reader learns of their roles in the village as they go about their daily lives, performing their tasks and sharing experiences in virtually mirror-like thoughts and actions. Incidentally, the girls were named on the day that life-giving water ended a long drought, thereby reviving the wilting corn.

As identical twins they represent the same tribal culture, but because of slight variances in their personalities, **they react differently to the advent of the white man (a French Jesuit missionary) in their village.** One girl is excited to hear about other places and other people, while her sister is fearful and cautious. One wants to travel and learn; the other is content to stay at home.

Their conversations and quarrels about the European newcomers will result in difficult life choices that will surely have profound psychological effects on the rest of their lives. In the case of identical twins, who by nature have a unique physical and spiritual bond, these effects may be especially stressful. Their ultimate choices (either to engage with the white man's culture or to avoid it) symbolize an overall **cultural and psychological divide**: the personal conflict between duty and desire. Can crucial differences between people be resolved completely or must each person learn to tolerate opposing opinions with respect and understanding?

Book 3, *Johannes van der Zee*, is the continuing story of the Dutch cabin boy who appeared in Book 1. From the deck of Adriaen Block's ship he had thrown his hat to Tail Feather as means of greeting. Book 3 begins three years later (1616) when Johannes is a sailor based in the **Dutch port of Hoorn**. From his perch high up in the mast, the boy directs his telescope at the frantic activity in the village, at the market stalls, and at the wharf where crew members are loading cargo onto his ship. As he sets sail to revisit the North River, the busy panorama of Hoorn recedes. It is a mercantile and cultural setting that later will offer sharp contrasts to the natural world of the people across the sea.

Vividly described between those two worlds is the **rough and tumble life on board *The Unicorn*,** (*De Eenhoorn*), where dangerous and life-threatening duties show no mercy to anyone not prepared. As no textbook rendition ever can, Book 3 describes the thrills and the horrors of an oceanic voyage in the early 17th century. It offers glimpses into the lives of the sailors: their quarreling during the lulls and their cruel punishments afterwards.

The nautical vocabulary is meant only to provide the flavor of a ship under way. (The *Landlubber* dictionary in the Reference Notes provides information about sailing terminology.) Book 3 also enlightens the reader about **religious persecution** in England and **religious tolerance** in the Dutch Republic. Reginald, the cabin boy, describes the objections of the Separatists and the Puritans to the practices of the Church of England.

After Johannes and Tail Feather meet again at the **Dutch trading post,** they form a friendship developed by attempts to communicate with hand signals. Invited to visit **Tahawus,** his friend's village, the sailor is astonished to find a functioning community that thrives not by money and mechanical inventions but by **ingenuity and hard work**; it is also one governed by strong tribal laws and values. He already knows from a winter endured three years earlier on an island with Captain Block that the river tribes are self-sufficient and helpful. Now he is amazed. If these people were so uncivilized (the original meaning of "savage") as the Europeans considered the Native Americans to be, then how could they devise such a well-organized community that could deal so well with seasonal survival issues? These included the procurement of food, shelter, clothing, and defense, as well as the associated concerns of soil conservation *(The Three Sisters),* the manufacture of tools and cooking pots from stones and clay, and economic prosperity through trade.

While walking about the village with Tail Feather's guidance and considerable hand-talking, the young Dutchman sees in these Mohawks examples of intelligence and creativity. Considering some shady commercial schemes prevalent among Dutch merchants and the disregard of the ship's captain for the well-being of his crew, Johannes eventually realizes that the "simple" forest dwellers may have a higher sense of **ethical behavior** than some of his own compatriots.

Cultural conflict surely happens when the affairs of the heart become involved. Awakens Corn, one of the twins, is attracted to her brother's guest, a man of another race, another language, another religion, and another culture. Her sister, Laughing Rain, respects the admonitions of the village elders, hoping to preserve their deep-rooted tribal values against foreign encroachment. Trouble brews! The Mohawks view the stranger as an interloper who threatens the racial purity of their clan. From his point of view, Johannes is bewildered that his pleasant outing with Awakens Corn could be construed so negatively.

Book 4, *Sky Flower*. As a small child, Sky Flower is a village favorite, pleasing to look at and hopelessly spoiled by her sisters. Because her skin tends to blister if exposed to the sun, her family does not expect her to perform many outside chores. Clan members consider her lazy and her behavior, inappropriate. As an adolescent, she accepts a position in the Dutch colony of Fort Orange (present-day Albany). There, she becomes a caregiver in charge of an ailing Dutch girl about her own age. Sky Flower then becomes a victim of the first calamity to befall the Native Americans since the incursions of the white man into their lands: the disease of **smallpox.** It is an event that changes her attitude and outlook for the future.

A survivor of this disease may experience the **psychological trauma** of a compromised identity. The scarred person, looking into the mirror and seeing a "stranger," may undergo a major loss of self-confidence. The trauma of being stared at, or even ostracized by peers, can take its toll emotionally. Sky Flower, however, is strong, resilient, and resourceful. She realizes that her survival now depends on how well she adjusts to the changing world and to her ability to compensate for her scarred body. This is a life lesson applicable to all people who become disfigured for any reason, whether minor or severe, and to children as well as adults.

Among the sociological aspects of Book 4 is the topic of **communal life, including housing and households**. Whereas Books 1, 2, and 3 portray in detail the palisaded village and the smoky longhouses of a Mohawk community, as well as the lodging styles of other tribes downriver, Book 4 highlights European communities. Sky Flower learns to adjust to a Dutch-style dwelling of a simple family in Fort Orange, then to a noisy tavern in multicultural New Amsterdam, and finally to an English manor house. In each place, the reader can visualize the furnishings of people in close confinement, their public and private living areas and perhaps even smell the aromas of cooking, whether over open pit or hearth. Most startling, and in contrast to all these places, is the city of London, a massive center of humanity where people live tightly confined in noisy, dirty, and smelly tenement houses and spend their days trying to survive as best they can. In time, Sky Flower will see how a city--despite its grand houses and wealth-- becomes inextricably identified with human desperation, disease, commerce, and crime.

Book 4 throws light on another sociological dimension: the **economic importance of a river for a community's growth and well-being.** Beverwyck is well-situated along the North River (that is, the Hudson). Ships from Holland now bring new settlers, animals, and goods acquired from other global ports including human cargo, too, enslaved people from Africa. **Sailing ships** such as the one that Tail Feather and his companions in Book 1 had viewed from their canoes, now, in Book 4, become regular visitors to this busy port. For the Mohawks and other Iroquois tribes living along the "Mohawk River" as well as the

Algonquin tribes along the "Hudson River," **canoes** are just as important as ships are for the Dutch. The trading of flint, copper, shells for wampum and other items, conducted by both river expeditions and by long distance runners overland, is vital to the well-being of all the woodland clans. The economic survival of a tribe, therefore, depends in part on the construction and repair of its canoes. The river serves as vital conduit for all communities, both Indigenous and European.

Economic growth depends also on adequate **food resources,** but the early Dutch settlers were not adept at hunting enough game to support their families. They had to import **domesticated animals** (horses, cattle, oxen, swine, and poultry, including chickens and geese), just to survive. Adapting to their new woodland environment was a difficult learning process for them, whereas native people, according to tribal lore, were at one with the natural world since its creation. The reader will remember in the earlier Books how important the **deer** and the **bear** were for the Iroquois. Now in Book 4 the contrast with the Europeans' perspective is clear. Animals in service to the villagers, such as horses, in no way resembled the Native Americans' respect for their animals and their prudent use of all the parts. (Later, during her stay in England, Sky Flower will assess the high value accorded to **horses,** not only as a means of transportation but as a means of pleasure for fox hunting and other forms of upper-class recreation.)

From a sociological perspective, Sky Flower finds in England the most egregious example of cultural differences: **social inequities**. While employed as a domestic servant in an English manor house, she is made aware of the **class distinctions in this household,** so different from the ways of her people: the disparity between the servant class and the nobility, including their separate expectations and duties, the subject of educating privileged children, the role of an impaired child in this culture— in this case, a child who cannot hear and does not speak—and finally, the role of religion and spiritual values for all concerned.

The Walsingham Manor House itself can be viewed as a **microcosm of 17th century English society**. Stemming from the medieval concept of class division (clergy, nobility, and serfs), and reinforced by the Great Chain of Being concepts of the Church of England, the household maintains the separation of family and servants. The irony, of course, is that as much as the noble family tries to stay "above the fray," it occasionally needs to interact with the servants below in order to maintain the status quo.

Several scenes present a realistic portrayal of this social division; for example, the one in the servants' kitchen when Sky Flower first arrives at the Manor House, and another in the formal dining room when she monitors the children's table manners. The food that looks so inviting on the elegant table has been meticulously prepared by servants supervised by the Chief Housekeeper. The "betters" enjoying the dinners are oblivious to the efforts by the "lessers" involved in the preparation: from gutting fish and making sauces to the washing and ironing of the table linen. A maid's candid remark is revealing: When asked by Sky Flower why eels, so common a food in Dutch Fort Orange, were never served at the Manor House, she replies: "Eels come from the mud. The Walsinghams think them hardly fit to eat, except, of course, by those who labor." Highlighting social division as well is the set of household rules for servants that Sky Flower remembers to add to her diary. Subservience to a higher order is not part of her Iroquois-Mohawk value system. She adds other examples of social divisions from the areas of recreation and education.

Among the servants two stand out: Kinshasa, the kitchen

maid, and Harold, the gardener. They are individuals from the non-dominant groups of people, those who help make up the multicultural landscape of Stuart England. Both characters tell their stories candidly and almost without emotion. Kinshasa's story is a peek into the devastating effects of the **African slave trade.** As a young child she was part of the human cargo sold in England to members of the privileged classes. Harold's story is one of **religious oppression**. It exemplifies the campaign by the Church of England to stamp out "heretical" versions of Christianity, especially those that would advocate the equal division of labor, a tenet upheld by the **Puritans**. Harold must therefore hide his Puritan faith for fear of persecution and death. The reader may remember in Book 3 the plight of Reginald and his parents who fled England for the same reasons.

Both servants find ways of adjusting to their lower status in the English hierarchy. Kinshasa grows up living according to English traditions and is resigned to it, as are, she indicates, all the other desperate, starving, and sick people she sees along the road to London and in the city. She may feel fortunate to know that a bed and a plate of food await her every day as long as she obeys the rules of conduct. Harold, a servant belonging to the outdoor staff at the manor, is sustained by his religion. Acceptance of one's fate, regardless of the circumstance, is demanded by God. And so, he, too, quietly acquiesces to the status quo regulated by the Church of England.

Sky Flower's reactions to all she sees and learns of social classes and economic disparity is one of disbelief. That such a system of values and traditions could exist seems appalling, for her own religion tells her just the opposite. No one expresses interest in her faith, while the Walsinghams consider her only a heathen. No matter how clever and helpful she is to the household, she remains an inferior servant. Recognizing the **hypocrisy and inequities** in much of English life, and recoiling from the disappointing behavior of a friend, the Mohawk girl resolves to return to her homeland. She will soon witness the devastating effects of European conquest on her own people.

The title of **Book 5,** *Mary Walsingham,* refers to the youngest daughter of an upper-class family in England. The Walsinghams live in a manor house in the parish of Littleton at the southernmost bend in the Thames. As a child who does not speak, Mary proves unmanageable. The duties of Sky Flower, brought over from New Amsterdam, are to work as a servant in the household and to make an unruly child civil and compliant.

Once she discovers that deafness (and not simple-mindedness) is the reason why Mary does not speak and behave as she is expected, Sky Flower resorts to her native culture to invent **hand-signals for communication,** just as various Native Americans from far-reaching lands used them to facilitate trading expeditions with each other. She also encourages Mary's interest in drawing animals and flowers.

Understandably, Sky Flower's abrupt departure from the Manor House has a devastating **psychological impact** on Mary. The girl is traumatized. The gift of a new-born foal gradually eases the loss of her best friend and teacher. Developing a close relationship to this special animal helps heal her wounded heart. She begins to spend time in the stables, grooming and caring for the animals. Although her parents consider such activities unnatural for a girl of noble lineage, they finally and reluctantly acknowledge the usefulness of these activities in their daughter's unique education. Mary's reaction to all these events is not any different from that of a hearing and speaking girl, showing that loss, grief, and solace are common to all kinds of individuals, "impaired" or not.

Mary's outlook becomes less self-centered as she learns about the **practical reality of commerce** and life beyond the Walsingham estate. After a difficult ocean voyage spent mostly below deck caring for animals, she comes to a Puritan household in **Hartford,** along the shore of the Connecticut River, and to a plantation barely three years old. It is far away from other more populated areas. Striving for historical accuracy, the author has identified Mary's hosts as the Adams family, whose house can be located on a map Hartford at that time. (Genealogical research into the actual family has provided, unfortunately, few facts beyond those of birth, marriage, and death dates).

Viewed from **a sociological perspective**, Mary soon realizes that her upper-class status means nothing in this Puritan household. There is **no servant class** here. The new daughter is expected to behave like any other family member for the greater good of the community. As she befriends the Adams children, she becomes an astute observer of Puritan customs and beliefs. She marvels, for example, at the absence of frivolity and gift-giving at Christmas. At the same time, she becomes aware of the pervasive influence of **religion, superstition, and witchcraft** in everyday life. (The reader may recall the horror of mob rule and superstition described in The Crucible, a play often read by high school students.) Mary's understanding of these factors, while naturally limited, is balanced by what she learns from Pieter (a Dutch trader based in New Netherland) about the **more open Dutch lifestyle** and by her earlier lessons from Sky Flower about **Mohawk beliefs of spirituality**. All communications with Mary are necessarily in writing, facial expressions, and gestures by hand.

There are **new health concerns** in Book 5. The maladies

afflicting the Adams children in this story could very well be those of young people today. But in the early 17th century health issues, especially those concerning physical and mental abnormalities, were often influenced by societal attitudes and prejudices. In Puritan neighborhoods, the fear of witchcraft always lurked at the back of one's mind and imagination, and that fear increased toward anyone deemed **"different."**

Rebecca Adams, fifteen going on sixteen years old, is a gifted poet. Nonetheless, her frequent and prolonged **migraine headaches** are making her into a recluse and even the subject of menacing gossip. She is at the point of becoming a social misfit, one whose outbursts of creative energy and then periods of melancholy could be construed as the work of the devil. Mary's clever ingenuity saves the day, so to speak, by alleviating this physical ailment and preventing an outbreak of **social hysteria in an age of witch-hunting**. The anguish that the Adams family experiences due to Rebecca's health problems gives way to the relief they feel when Mary's strategies work.

Thomas's odd personality might be viewed today as a case of **Asperger's Syndrome**, a form of autism that may have an anti-social dimension to a greater or lesser degree. Capable of completing manual tasks, Thomas remains an intelligent and dependable member of the household. At the same time he desires solitude and time to spend with objects found during his frequent wanderings in the forest and along the riverbanks. Unlike Mary who cannot speak, Thomas has no wish to do so if not necessary. But when he does speak, he prefers to talk about his treasured findings, amazing his listeners with detailed facts and descriptions. At times he reveals a curiosity about the girl from England who has come to live in his home. As she senses his growing interest in her, Mary decides to enlist Rebecca in her plan to help the boy become more open and confident, and more comfortable with other people.

Baby John's **foot deformity**, if not corrected early in life, presents a life-long obstacle to normal weight-bearing. It necessarily puts the body weight along the outside edge of the foot, causing pain, a serious limp, and limitations on one's ability to walk. With physical activities severely curtailed, the child without treatment for a clubfoot would have a difficult time growing up in an agricultural society dependent on manual labor.

Mary offers a solution to the distraught parents. She writes to Goodman Adams that John need not become a farmer. He could have a productive life simply by using his intellect and drawing upon his spiritual strength. In his destiny as a Puritan, the boy would need, in any case, to rely upon his inner resources and talents, thereby learning how best to serve God and his community, whether as preacher or teacher. The help of Reverend Hooker, the plantation's leader, will undoubtedly be needed.

For today's student there is a "take-away" lesson from all of Mary's efforts to remedy the problems in the Adams family. Offering compassion, help, and friendship to someone afflicted with a strange "problem" can have a positive **psychological impact** on both the recipient as well as the provider. In addition, when that provider or caregiver is also an "impaired" person, his or her own self-esteem increases in the effort. Mary's efforts to help others indicate a milestone in her road to maturity.

C.

The English Language Arts Curriculum

Literature and Language

As literature, The River Quintet series could be assessed as educationally appropriate for the **seventh-grade level,** at a minimum, **to the twelfth-grade level.** Encompassing a wide range of topics, such as travel by water, wilderness survival, biology, botany, geology, lifestyles of the privileged and the impoverished, and religious and ethical values, the series offers stories that dramatically enhance the **interdisciplinary** studies of English, history, geography, health, and science. It also offers insight into specific health-related issues, giving the reader a view of 17th century life rarely elaborated upon in social studies textbooks. Diseases and injuries, as well as the aberrations of mental and physical health are represented through various characters. The problems experienced by these characters may also be similar and relevant to the readers themselves, an aspect that may lead to class discussions.

Language. In Books 4 and 5 the author has modified English vocabulary and syntax in keeping with the historical framework of the novels and the linguistically unique situations of two main characters. The reader should be reminded that Sky Flower's native language is Mohawk (an Iroquois language), and her second language is Dutch. Mary's first language is "hand-speak," that is, sign language in the style of Native Americans. She learns later to communicate in English through handwriting. Although their words and sentence structures may seem odd or wrong to the contemporary reader, they are intended to be so. These words may also seem imperfect from the point of view of a native speaker of English, but they are understandable, **given the difficulty of both a non-native speaker and a deaf girl in acquiring experience of the written word.**

Various "misspellings" should give a flavor of the seventeenth century but not enough to impede the reader's comprehension. Teachers should explain that the purpose of such words is to provide visual cues that would highlight the historical framework of the novel and reflect as well Sky Flower's own education by the Walsingham tutors. In fact, the word *yeere* in the first diary entry and the first word of the *Memoirs*, "snowe," prepare the reader for a journey back in time. The following list offers a sampling of these differently spelled or out-of- fashion words.

> *aasoon, affaires, after-noone, againe, aire, beganne, beginne, cleer, cleerly, coale, countery, cryes, deepe, deepely, doe (do), dores, downe, durst- (dared), deyd, earlie, faireness, feare, fearefull, fogge, foure, graine, greene,haile huneysuckle, knowne, methinks, myst, nearely, neereby, neereness, neerest, neering, pye, sayle,*

sayled, shawle, snowe, snowemelt, snowes, sommer(s),
storme, stormie, streame, sunne, sunnie, tooke, tyme,
unfaireness, whilst, winde, writ, yeere

In terms of the level of **reading difficulty**, the vocabulary throughout the series could be assessed as moderately easy to moderately challenging. For students at the lowest grade level, or for students with reading challenges, the teacher might like to create pre-reading vocabulary lists. These should be introduced to the students before actual reading of the text begins. Such an introduction helps students understand the meaning of specific words, thus facilitating comprehension later when the story is read or discussed in class.

Literary Aspects

The five books of The River Quintet are set on two continents and in three culturally different societies. Rather than presenting the intricate stories of multiple branches of a family, such as in a saga, the "RQ" concentrates on one Iroquois-Mohawk family: four generations in the space of five books. Its narrative reach is geographically wide, and its timespan covers more than eighty years. It has a cast of several major characters, each one with a unique story. The five novels are connected by the characters' common family links and their relationship to other people in interpersonal situations.

Theme.

The five novels explore the theme of **maturation,** or simply put, growing up or coming-of-age. Starting with **Book 1,** the story of Tail Feather, this theme will foreshadow the life stories of characters in the succeeding books. In these, the theme expands at an ever-widening scale, with each Book presenting the characters with increasingly complex issues. In this regard, one can view Tail Feather's down-river journey to the ocean as a metaphor of self-awareness and the process of his maturation. His emotional development foreshadows issues to come.

In **Book 2,** his sisters deal with a moral conflict as each one struggles to make a choice between duty and desire—about what she ought to do and what she would like to do. Two values hang in the balance: the preservation of her culture and satisfaction on a personal level. The choice for Laughing Rain is easy: her happiness depends on the integrity of her heritage. For her sister, there are wider horizons of existential import. The burgeoning free spirit in Awakens Corn demands to be heard!

In **Book 3** the theme widens as Johannes deals with conflicts and misconceptions based on the long-held prejudices of his European culture. How he resolves these issues is his life's lesson. He will soon be able to match his talents with realistic aspirations, rejoin his community, and plan for his future. But all this comes with newly-revised opinions of the "forest people" across the sea and his own compatriots.

In **Book 4** Sky Flower changes from being a self-centered child into an outreaching adult able to assess the cultural values of both continents.

In **Book 5** non-hearing and non-speaking Mary perfects a form of communication using hand gestures and letters. She also develops a sense of emotional independence as she adjusts to life in the hearing-world. With compassion, she learns to look beyond herself to the needs of others around her and then to think of her own path forward.

In summary: The process of simply growing up reveals opportunities for fictional characters to make life choices, either great or small. In Book 1, an adolescent tries to overcome his feelings of insecurity. In Book 2, two young girls struggle to solve a moral conflict. In Book 3, a young man confronts his own prejudices and unrealistic personal goals. In Book 4 a young woman learns what is important to her. Finally, in Book 5, a deaf girl learns to relate to the world around her.

All these characters experience situations through which they eventually gain knowledge about themselves. Such recognition is the first step towards maturity. Seen from this perspective, each book of The River Quintet series can be viewed as a **bildungsroman** or novel of an adolescent's unsteady and often turbulent transition into the world of adults.

Foreshadowing
Examples from the novels:

1. An unwise or impulsive decision that leads to pain and disappointment is the first hint at unwelcome repercussions around the corner. In Book 1 Tail Feather's chase after the Running Man will end in misery and embarrassment just as, in Book 2, Awakens Corn flight into the mountains, looking for solitude and relief, will end in pain and loneliness. In Book 3, when Awakens Corn and Johannes enjoy a woodland stroll and miss their curfew, they will reap the displeasure of her clan. In Book 4 Sky Flower's sudden decision to leave her post for a

romantic pursuit will result in deception and grief. In Book 5 Mary's decision to join Pieter for a day's outing will cause great upset in the Adams family.

2. The nighttime stories about far-away monsters in Book 1 will materialize as real (e.g., the whale) and natural (e.g., the waterfall at Cohoes), as Tail Feather will discover on his journey.

3. Transporting animals onboard a ship: In Book 3 Reginald's duties as cabin boy include feeding the animals and cleaning out their stalls. In Book 5 when Lord Walsingham agrees to send the horses overseas, the reader might remember Reginald's troubles on *The Unicorn* and might suspect that Mary will have similar duties. This time, though, there will be much more description of the difficult tasks and the hardships involved in tending to large animals on a long sea voyage.

4. Sky Flower's talent for nurturing is first evident in Fort Orange when she looks after Katrina, a girl with consumption. The reader should not be surprised later when she cares for and teaches another girl. Sky Flower will eventually find a permanent job as teacher in a one-room schoolhouse.

Fictional rather than factual introduction to the book

A fictional publication history serves as an introduction to *Sky Flower*. This section takes the form of a series of letters between the current owners of the *Memoirs* and potential book publishers. Part I, *The Publication History of the Memoirs of Sky Flower*, is concluded with the addendum by Gladys Eddy. It serves to indicate the length of time (approximately sixty years, from 1964 onward) needed for the public to express interest in the lives of Indigenous Americans. The acceptance of the manuscript comes at a time when historians are attempting to address the issues of racial stereotyping of all minorities and the social and legal inequities they have faced ever since the European conquest of the Americas. The *Publication History* also underscores the passing of years between the 17th century and the contemporary era. Prestley Press recognizes that old crumbling papers found in the ruins of what may have been a mountain cabin could be of great interest to people today, in this case, to young people. This unique foreword serves to make archeology and history become meaningful or, in other words, **to create a living history in the imagination of today's young adults.**

Format of the diary

Normally one writes a diary to record the day's events. In Book 4 Sky Flower does that but also adds much more. She uses her diary to record her memories of the past, hoping that someday someone might be interested in reading about her unusual life. In effect, she, born in 1613, starts in 1692 to write her MEMOIRS.

By writing in the first person singular, Sky Flower looks back over a half-century and draws attention to the effects that the arrival of Europeans had on her own life as well as the lives of other clan members. She tells her story, as she remembers it, while at the same time relating events happening around her at the time of writing. This format allows **two stories** to be told, **one of the past and one of the present time**. While readers may find such alternating narration confusing or at least disconcerting, the style offers a graphic description of the character's lonely and difficult life in the mountains. The reader cannot help but contrast Sky Flower's current circumstances with the past stages of her life.

Format of the letter

Book 2 is the first story to introduce the personal letter. As used here, it is a time-saving method that allows the author to convey past events quickly without having to describe them as they happen. In his letter to his superior in France, Brother André Benoît relates information about his arrival in Port Royal, New France, his journey up the Canada River, and his efforts to spread the message of Christianity to the Wyandots, Mi'kmaqs, and Mohawks. Brother André writes with a certain degree of pride about his exaggerated accomplishments during this religious mission and his endurance throughout his trek through the mountains. The European feeling of **cultural superiority** over the "savages" is evident. The letter does not reflect the skepticism of the people who heard his "Message of Joy." In this letter, moreover, the reader can recognize the extent of the **"New World" exploration** already undertaken by Samuel de Champlain, and before him, Jacques Cartier, many years before Henry Hudson ever sailed into the great bay below the island of the *Mannahatta* people.

In Books 4 and 5 the letter serves as a necessary tool which connects the deaf and mute protagonist with the hearing world. Ever since Sky Flower introduced the written word as a technique of communication, it has been an essential part of her student's education. In Book 5 Mary becomes proficient enough to exchange letters with her father and later with Jeremy Adams.

There are instances when a letter conveys a personal life-altering decision. Reactions by the recipients are different in each case. In Book 5 when Sky Flower writes that she will be leaving the manor house, Mary is heartbroken, indeed devastated. A year later, Mary, herself, writes to Rebecca of her decision to leave Hartford. The young poet accepts the news with grace and understanding. In the last three chapters, letters between Mary and Pieter provide the dual rationale (pro and con) that Mary needs to make the biggest decision of her life.

Character Development

As the main characters in the series deal with both positive and negative events in their lives, they gradually experience psychological transformations: moving from a focus inward to a focus outward. They learn to rely on their talents and inner strengths and not to let their "limitations" hinder their goals.

In **Books 1, 2 and 3** the characters **Tail Feather, Awakens Corn and Johannes** learn to view themselves critically in the light of newly gained knowledge of other cultures. With a better understanding themselves they can return to their villages with a new sense of purpose and outlook.

Books 4 and 5 together offer more opportunities for the two main characters to evaluate what they see and experience. The author expands their stories to allow for their reactions to various events and circumstances. Through the stylistic features of the letter and diary entries, they "give voice" to their feelings and opinions. Accordingly, one can make the following analyses of not only each of these protagonists but of the novels in general:

Book 4, *Sky Flower*. The fourth book presents a story of tragedy and resilience, heartbreak, and strength, all the aftermath of the European conquest of the Mohawk girl's own natural world. Students today should see in the character of Sky Flower not only a **strong and courageous girl** but also a **spirited survivor of a new world order**. Lessons learned from past mistakes and from observations of European society help guide her path. As a woman she finds that her life's work must reflect both the new knowledge of Europe and the ethical and natural values of her own people. Although she becomes a teacher in a Dutch community,

Sky Flower remains at heart an Iroquois historian who treasures her heritage.

Book 5, *Mary Walsingham,* presents a still deeper look into the psyche of its principal character. The author gives the English girl plenty of space to reflect on her changing world. Of all the books in the series, this one is the most poignant. Through poetry, written descriptions of people and places and the vivid imagery of nature, the author tries to convey the physical world as only a deaf and mute person would experience it: through written words, gestures and the senses of touch, smell, taste, and sight.

Once a lonely and misunderstood child, Mary becomes a young woman able to know what is happening around her. Her emergence from a state of withdrawal coincides with the development of her artistic talent and special ability to relate to animals. She takes on challenges that would be daunting even for a hearing girl of her social status. Her determination to save her horse from abusive training initiates a bold mindset that challenges the prescribed norms of female behavior. In fact, while sitting in the filthy bilge of the ship, she feels free and empowered. The irony is that she, as a person with a disability, believes herself to be in a better place than all the other English girls of her background. With growing self-confidence and resourcefulness Mary then tackles the issues troubling the Puritan family in Hartford.

Having helped both the Adams children and a neighboring family, Mary now can think about her own situation. An unexpected intrusion is a passion of the heart: her infatuation with the Dutch trader. Book 5 will end as Mary struggles to make a difficult decision. Whatever her choice of action, it will have momentous implications for the rest of her life. It will be the decision of a woman with a newly found sense of independence and a will to take control of her life. Indeed, she puts into action the message in that fateful letter written by her mentor two years earlier. Like Sky Flower, Mary learns a lesson of resilience in the face of adversity. She learns an **existential lesson of empowerment.** Quite simply stated, **Mary Walsingham is a true hero, a young woman who has come of age.**

Series Summary

Beginning with the unfolding panorama of the natural world and the cultures of North American woodland tribes, the series chronicles the lives of Mohawk siblings and their friendships with a Dutch boy and an English girl. These teenagers learn to recognize prejudices in themselves and others, to overcome whatever "deficits" others see in them, and to develop a sense of self-worth. At the same time, they learn to respect, if not always agreeing with, people of different viewpoints.

Presenting a contrast to what these young people may see as baffling in their own or other cultures is the dominant role of nature, whether it be a powerful ocean storm or the delicate leaf of a tree. Indeed, the natural world has a vital place in The River Quintet. In Books 1-3 it is shown to be the life source of the Indigenous peoples. In Book 5, through a horse, a red bird, and a gemstone called almandine, it helps a deaf girl understand the world about her. On the other hand, the frequent disrespect of the natural world by European cultures is made evident in Book 4.

As the series comes full circle, the relationship of one character to another becomes clear. The last two books reveal answers to questions that may have puzzled the reader: the fate of Tail Feather's family members (Book 4), and the connection between Pieter and Sky Flower (Book 5). There are no answers regarding Awakens Corn's life after Tahawus, the story behind Lionel's disappearance, and the outcome of Mary's big decision. Like Sky Flower who wonders for years what happened to Mary, the reader, too, has questions. These mysteries, however, are left to the reader's imagination.

The Reference Section

In the words of the author, each of four of the novels, **(Books 1, 2, 3, and 5),** is divided into a third-person narrative called the Story, followed by an educational addendum called Notes About The Story. Book 4 is divided into a first-person narrative in the form of Memoirs, and an educational addendum called a Historical Framework.

    BOOKS 1, 2, 3, and 5. The **NOTES ABOUT THE STORY** contain information about topics referred to throughout the novels. They include: 1. historical and social aspects (cultures and values); 2. biological aspects (flora and fauna); 3. health-related aspects (physical and mental issues); 4. geographic features (mountains, rivers, and forests); 5. geologic features (glaciers, caverns, and rocks) and finally, 6. oceanic travel. The NOTES are not meant to be encyclopedic in content; they are meant, instead, to offer interesting explanations or extensions of a given topic.

    It should be stated, nevertheless, that *reading the NOTES is optional.* The information presented is not vital to the overall comprehension of each story. Students with reading difficulties may benefit from hearing selected information presented informally by the teacher or by other students. Classroom focus should be on the plots and, ideally, lively discussions of the issues involved. A **LIST OF NOTES** appears at the end of each novel. Identified are the chapter locations, number and title of each Note. **BOOK 4** is followed by a **HISTORICAL FRAMEWORK** for understanding the background of the story. This section consists of an overview of events in 17th century Europe (indicating, as well, their relevancy to the plot of Book 4) and a global timeline of a few historical facts in conjunction with the events in the protagonist's life, **1613-1692**. It is plausible that Sky Flower's date of death occurs soon after the last diary entry. The Lists and Historical Framework, appearing at the end of their respective novels, serve the *Companion Guide* as **convenient reference aids.**

1. List of Notes

Book 1: *Tail Feather*

Chapter	Note	Title
1	1	Native Americans
	2	The Stockade
	3	The Setting
	4	The Clan
	5	The Runner
	6	Turkey-Feathered Clothes
	7	Sassafras
	8	Copper
	9	Lake Ontario
	10	Niagara Falls
	11	Game with Leather Stick
	12	Howe Caverns
	13	The Black Robes
	14	Wampum
	15	The League of the Iroquois
2	16	The Longhouse
	17	Activities in Winter
	18	Telling Stories
	19	Language
3	20	The Family
	21	Hunting
	22	Food in Winter
	23	Clothing
	24	Pottery
	25	Weaving

Chapter	Note	Title
7	56	Journey Food
	57	Wood
	58	Building a Canoe
	59	Festivals
	60	The Sweat Lodge
	61	Beaver Tail Soup
	62	Cedar Tea
	63	The Smoking Pipe
	64	Dance
	65	Rhythms
8	66	Moccasins
	67	The Loon
9	68	Canoe Handling
	69	Rapids
	70	Woodland Birds
10	71	Hudson River Gorge
	72	Linking a Canoe
	73	Moose
	74	Repairing a Canoe
	75	Evergreen Trees
11	76	Blue Ledges
	77	The Osprey
	78	The Speckled Trout
	79	The Snapping Turtle
	80	The Cougar
	81	The Butterfly
	82	Beauty
	83	Things Bittersweet
12	84	Mohicans / Mahicans
	85	Rockwell Falls

Chapter	Note	Title
	86	The Fate of Captives
	87	Potholes
	88	Bone Fracture
13	89	Waterfalls
	90	Maternal Instincts
14	91	The Mohawk River
	92	Cohoes Falls
	93	Rainbow
	94	Clouds
15	95	Catskill Mountains
	96	Castle Island
	97	The White-Tailed Fawn
	98	The Estuary
16	99	The Marsh
	100	Trail Food
	101	Cattails
	102	The Comb
	103	The Ramapoughs
	104	Childbirth
	105	Twins
	106	The Snake
	107	The Moon
	108	The Great Bear
	109	The Twin Stars
17	110	Middens
	111	Regrowth of Land
	112	Striped Bass
	113	Portable Water
	114	Lacrosse
	115	The Wappingers

Chapter	Note	Title
	116	Witch Hazel
	117	The Poultice
	118	Black Flies
	119	Bug Repellent
18	120	The Shad Tree
	121	The Hudson Highlands
	122	Pollepel Island
	123	Breakneck Mountain
	124	Storm King Mountain
	125	Hair Styles
	126	Constitution Island
	127	West Point
	128	War Canoes
	129	The Thunderstorm
	130	Rough Water Canoeing
	131	Hypothermia
	132	The Popcorn Surprise
19	133	Shad
	134	Popolopen Creek
	135	The Muskrat
	136	Hand Signals
	137	Courtesies
	138	The Sturgeon
	139	The Munsees
	140	Dugout Canoes
	141	The Tulip Tree
	142	Personal Hygiene
20	143	Sing Sing
	144	Granite
	145	The Tappan Zee

Chapter	Note	Title
	176	Making Wampum
	177	Words
	178	Long Distance Commerce
	179	Albinism
	180	The Owl
24	181	New York Harbor
	182	The Harbor Islands
	183	The Narrows
	184	Coney Island
	185	The Canarsees
	186	The Horizon
	187	Sperm Whales
	188	The East River
	189	The Brooklyn Bridge
	190	Roosevelt Island
	191	Hell's Gate
	192	Highbridge
	193	Kingsbridge
	194	Spuyten Duvil and The Harlem River Ship Canal
	195	The Island of Manhattan
25	196	Outcasts
	197	The Gift
	198	Names for the Hudson River

Book 2: *Laughing Rain and Awakens Corn*

Chapter	Note	Title
1	1	Henderson Lake
	2	Hudson River
	3	The Iroquois
	4	Mount Marcy
	5	Water-With-No-End
	6	Cattails
	7	Coyote
	8	Domesticated Wolf
	9	Roles of Gender
	10	Village
2	11	The Three Sisters
	12	Chief
	13	Tobacco Leaves
	14	Story of Creation
3	15	Tools
	16	Twins
	17	Names
4	18	Loon
	19	Porcupine
	20	Peepers
	21	Woodland Scents
	22	Black Bear
	23	Elk
5	24	Rainbow
6	25	Midden
	26	Wolf
8	27	Missionaries
	28	Religions
	29	Baptism
10	30	Maize
12	31	Basketmaking
	32	Clay Pot
13	33	Water Strider
	34	Mirror
	35	Spider Web
	36	Hunting

Chapter	Note	Title
	37	Beaver / Dam Building
	38	Jewelweed
	39	Bear Cubs
	40	Big Chill
	41	Rattlesnake
	42	Lost in the Woods
	43	Blackberries
14	44	Council House
	45	Dislocated Shoulder
15	46	Marriage
	47	String Beads / Wampum
16	48	Lenapes
17	49	Crooked Tongues
	50	Saint Lawrence River
	51	Hiawatha
	52	Onondagas
	53	Mohawk River
	54	Oneidas
	55	The Iroquois Great League of Peace and Power
	56	Mi'kmaq
	57	Timeline
	58	Canoe
	59	Quebec
18	60	Sky Hunt
	61	Wolf Pup
19	62	Sparkling Stones
	63	Healing Arts
	64	Concept of Death
	65	Milky Way
	66	Cornhusk Doll
	67	Funeral Rites
	68	Turtle Shell Moon Clock
20	69	Stories from the Journey to Water-With-No-End

Book 3: *Johannes van der Zee*

Chapter	Note	Title of Note
1	1	Landlubber's Dictionary
	2	Hoorn
	3	Dutch East India Company
	4	Telescope
	5	Weathercock
	6	Wilden
	7	New Netherland
	8	Golden Age of Maritime Holland
	9	Ship's Officers
	10	Fluyt
	11	Unicorn
	12	Shipmaster Adriaen Block
	13	Sea Shanties
	14	The Zuider Zee
	15	World Events of 1616
2	16	Life for the Common Person
3	17	Trade Winds
	18	The Rogue Wave
	19	The Crew
	20	Shipboard Cuisine
	21	Shallop
	22	Barents Sea
	23	The Northern Lights
	24	Religious Tensions
	25	Windmills
4	26	Tar
	27	Maurice of Nassau, Prince of Orange
	28	The Sandglass
	29	Monsters of the Sea
	30	Knots
	31	The Dutch: Guild Members and Others
	32	*Onrust*
	33	Tulips
5	34	Discipline at Sea

Chapter	Note	Title of Note
	35	Chiprock Reach
	36	Dead Man's Breath
	37	Cross-staff
	38	Position of the Earth
	39	Amsterdam
	40	Fur Trade
	41	Scurvy
	42	Compass
6	43	Storm at Sea
7	44	Ship's Log
8	45	Dutch Luck
	46	Cape Cod
	47	Lower New York Bay
	48	The Narrows
	49	Upper New York Bay
	50	New Amsterdam
	51	Washington Heights
	52	Harlem River
	53	Palisades
9	54	Chiprock Reach, Again
	55	Saw Mill River
	56	Tappan Zee
	57	Sing Sing
	58	Croton Point
	59	Hudson Highlands
	60	Leadsman
	61	Claverack
10	62	Fort Nassau
12	63	Mahicans (Mohicans)
14	64	Mohawks
15	65	*Sint Nicolaas/Sinterklaas*
	66	Cabin Fever
	67	Magnifying Glass
	68	Firearms
18	69	Cohoes Falls
19	70	*Castor canadensis*
	71	Glens Falls
	72	Rockwell Falls
	73	Blue Ledges

Chapter	Note	Title of Note
	74	Harmen van den Bogaert
20	75	Chief
	76	United Provinces of the Netherlands
	77	Dutch Artists
21	78	Calamity Brook
	79	Venus
23	80	*Toxicodendron radicans*
	81	*Mephitis mephitis*
	82	*Impatiens scapiflora*
24	83	Spring Floods
25	84	Aalsmeer
26	85	The Dream Quest

Book 5: *Mary Walsingham*

Chapter	Note	Title
2	1	Littleton
	2	Magpie
	3	Puppet Show
	4	Toys & Games of 17th Century England
	5	Insanity: Changing Attitudes
	6	Hard-of-Hearing With Aging
	7	The River Ash
	8	Horse: Attraction
	9	New Amsterdam
3	10	Pocahontas
	11	Smallpox: Immunity
	12	Gwendolyn: Origin of Name
	13	Sir Francis Drake
	14	Deafness: Children
	15	Chinese Vase
	16	The Royal College of Physicians
	17	Deafness: Early Attitudes
	18	Deafness: Traditional Treatment
	19	Deaf: Education
	20	Prism
	21	The River Thames
	22	Orangery
	23	Horse: Domestication
	24	Blacksmith
	25	Vibrations
	26	Iron Horse
4	27	Foal
	28	Horse
	29	Staines
	30	Windsor Castle
	31	Puritans: Plymouth and the Massachusetts Bay Colony
	32	Pudding Lane
	33	*Countrey Contentments or The English Huswife*

Chapter	Note	Title
	34	Quayside: London
	35	Animals: Ship Transport
	36	Gervase Markham (B. 1568 – D. 1637)
	37	Fishers Island
	38	Connecticut River
	39	Leadsman or Plumb Lead Line
	40	Bodkin Rock
5	41	Fainting
	42	Hartford: The Beginning
	43	Nutmeg
	44	Food
	45	Horses: North America
6	46	Colonial House
	47	Diaspora
	48	Reverend Thomas Hooker
	49	Oxen and Horses
	50	First People
	51	Migraine
	52	Colonial Women
	53	Historical Data
	54	Dutch Fort and Trading Post: House of Good Hope
	55	Neighbors: The Dutch and the English
	56	Meetinghouse
	57	Connecticut Constitution
	58	Dutch Sloop
9	59	Spring Peepers
	60	Bathing
	61	Hartford: The City
	62	Flood
	63	Quinsy
10	64	Almandine
	65	Witch
	66	John Donne
	67	Cavern versus Cave
	68	Sonnet
11	69	Horse: Leg Injury
	70	Asperger's Syndrome
	71	Delftware Pottery
	72	Grass

2. Historical Framework, Book 4

A. 17th Century Europe and the Life of Sky Flower

During Sky Flower's lifetime the European stage is dominated by major religious and political warfare both on sea and on land. Naval battles between European nations, and between European merchant ships and pirates along the Barbary coast continue throughout the century. In the Mediterranean Sea confrontations between Venetian, Spanish, Dutch, Portuguese, French and English ships and those of the Ottoman Empire occur constantly. Settlements along the Atlantic Ocean and North Sea are also vulnerable to attacks, and even the island of Lundy in the Bristol Channel becomes a haven for Ottoman pirates. Villages in Cornwall and Devon become frequent targets of their raids.

Pirates or "corsairs" of all ethnicities capture not only valuable cargos but people from coastal towns to be sold as slaves or ransomed. Captured Christians often convert to Islam to save their own lives. Captured Muslims, too, often become Christians for the same reason. Some English who helped the privateer Francis Drake defeat The Spanish Armada in 1588 become pirates themselves. **Sky Flower's voyages to and from England are undertaken against this perilous backdrop. The risk of capture and death at the hands of pirates as well as the theft of cargo always cause grave concerns for those aboard any ship. While the Mohawk girl might be unaware of all these dangers, the captain, the crew, and the investors in the mercantile shipping trade certainly would not be. In the home of an English noble family, Sky Flower will learn about another aspect of oceanic travel: the European involvement in the African slave trade.**

On the continent, the first half of the 17th century is dominated by conflicts between the Catholic forces of Austria and Spain and the Protestant forces led by the Dutch in their War of Independence and by the Swedes under King Gustavus Adolphus. Catholics consider the Calvinists (Huguenots), Lutherans, and other independent sects to be heretics, worthy of punishment by the ongoing Inquisition. Protestant groups, on the other hand, condemn Roman Catholics and members of the Church of England as "Papists" who, they claim, defy the true tenets of Christianity. Hypocrisy, cruelty, revenge, and superstition are the hallmarks of religious fervor at this time. **Sky Flower is first exposed to some of these problems during her conversations with Bertrand, a prisoner on the ship heading to England, and later with Harold, a Puritan gardener in England.**

In the second half of the century peace prevails in the Dutch Republic, giving rise to the Golden Age of Science and the Arts. In England, however, chaos continues. The monarchy is overthrown, then replaced by Parliamentarians under Cromwell, and is finally restored. **Sky Flower will learn of these political events long after she returns to her homeland.**

B. Global Timeline 1613-1692

Year - (*Sky Flower's Age, Location and Personal Event*)
- Global Event(s)

1613 (*Birth of Sky Flower, Tahawus, Adirondack Mountains*)
Captain Adriaen Block sails up the *Noordrivier* (Hudson River) in his ship, *Tijger*.

1614 *(under age 1, Tahawus. Sky Flower is baptized by a Jesuit missionary.)*
Construction of a ship, the *Onrust*, during the winter on what is today called Manhattan Island. (The *Tijger* had been destroyed in a fire.) Block uses the new ship to explore Long Island Sound up to Rhode Island, including the Connecticut River. Believing that he has found an island, he names it *Rood* (red) *Eyelandt,* due to its red clay soil. The British later change the name to Rhode Island. He also discovers and names Block Island.

1620 *(age 7, Tahawus)*
English Separatists establish a colony in Plymouth, Massachusetts.

1621 (age 8, Tahawus)
Eleven African men are brought to New Amsterdam as slaves of the Dutch West India Company.

1623 *(age 10, Tahawus)*
English colonists in Jamestown, Virginia kidnap Pocahontas, daughter of a Powhatan chief.

1624 *(age 11, Tahawus)*
1. Pocahontas converts to Christianity and marries the English planter, John Rolph, in Jamestown.
2. Dutch traders settle first on an island in New York Harbor, keeping cattle and constructing a fort and a sawmill. They call it *Noten Eylandt,* adapting the Lenape name of *Paggunuch*, which refers to the island's abundant nut trees (chestnut, oak, and hickory). The English call the island Nutten until 1874 when they rename it Governors Island.

1626 *(age 13, Tahawus)*
1. Pieter Minuit purchases Manhattan Island from the local Canarsees for a pittance. Dutch settlers call it *Nieuw* (New) *Amsterdam*.
2. English fishermen plying the northeastern coast begin a settlement called *Naumkeag*, named after a local Indigenous tribe. Settlers will soon change that name. (See note 2 for year 1627.)

1627 *(age 14, Fort Orange, New Netherland. Cares for a sick girl, Katrina van Stroomer.)*
1. On Aug. 29 the ship *Bruynvisch*, owned by the Dutch West India Company, brings many more enslaved Africans to New Amsterdam.
2. Emigrants from the Massachusetts Bay Colony move to the *Naumkeag* settlement and rename it Salem, the Hebrew word for peace.

1628 *(age 15, New Amsterdam, now New York City. Works as a tavern maid.)*
England grants a royal charter to the Massachusetts Bay Colony. Puritans from the Colony settle in Salem.

1629 *(age 16, Littleton, England. Begins work as laundry maid on the Walsingham estate.)*
The reign of King Charles I begins in England. His insistence on the "divine right of kings" clashes sharply with Parliament's authority of government, which will eventually lead to the English Civil War.

1630 *(age 17, Littleton and Shepperton, England. Begins work as child-minder and governess of the Walsingham children.)*
1. In the spring one thousand Puritans from Boston, England sail to the Massachusetts Bay Colony, arriving first in Salem, but soon

relocating to Charlestown. Reverend John Winthrop is appointed Governor. Within six years the number of Puritans increases to seventeen thousand.

2. The Dutch West Indies Company establishes a sugar-growing plantation in New Holland (the area today known as Brazil). After fourteen years and many battles on sea, the Dutch are forced out by the Portuguese and Spanish.

3. Anthony Janszoon van Salee, son of a Muslim Dutch pirate at Lundy Island, settles peacefully as a colonist in New Amsterdam.

1631 (age 18, Littleton, England)
The Massachusetts Bay Colony establishes the settlements of Newtowne and Trimount, later renamed Cambridge and Boston.

1633 (age 20, Littleton, England)
1. The Inquisition in Rome convicts Galileo of heresy for having published his scientific findings about the universe, which claim that the planets orbit the sun.

2. English settlers in Virginia establish Middle Plantation, a site later renamed Williamsburg.

1634 (age 21, Littleton, England)
Settlers arrive in present-day Maryland, a colony proposed by George Calvert, Lord of Baltimore. Championing religious tolerance for all religions, this colony would become a haven for harassed Catholics in England.

1635 (age 22, Littleton and London, England)
The Colony of Newtown (later named Hartford) on the Connecticut River is founded by Reverend Thomas Hooker and his Puritan followers.

1636 *(age 23, Littleton and London, England. Meets Lionel, the actor.)*
1. Harvard College is established in Newtowne (later called Cambridge) to train young men for the clergy. A major stimulus comes from a grant bestowed at the death of a thirty-one-year-old minister, John Harvard. He leaves an estate of a few thousand dollars in today's currency, and four hundred books. The college boasts of having the first printing press in the colonies.
2. Roger Williams, a preacher, is expelled from the Massachusetts Bay Colony for his liberal beliefs concerning religion. In Providence, Rhode Island he begins a settlement dedicated to religious tolerance.

1637 *(age 24, Newcastle-upon-Tyne, York, Plymouth; Boston, New Amsterdam, Beverwyck (Albany). Leaves the manor house and then England entirely.)*
René Descartes publishes "Discourses of the Method of Rightly Conducting One's Reason and of Seeking the Truth in the Sciences." His idea shakes the established minds of the times: all previous information on the natural world should be discarded. Learning should start over by means of scientific processes.

1638 *(age 25, Tahawus. Unites with her brother, Tail Feather, and others in the family.)*
English colonists attack the Pequots in or around Mystic, Connecticut. Many members of the tribe are killed and others scatter.

1639 *(age 26, Peebles Island)*
Anthony Janszoon van Salee joins other settlers to create the village of Breukelen (Brooklyn,) named after a village in the Dutch province of Utrecht. A few years later he will receive a patent for a large estate near *Conyne Eylandt* (Coney Island).

1641 *(age 28, Peebles Island. Begins teaching in her new schoolhouse.)*
Dutch lawyer, Adriaen van der Donck, arrives in Beverwyck. He represents Kiliaen van Rensselaer, a jewel merchant in Amsterdam and the holder of a huge land grant on both sides of the North (Hudson) River. Van der Donck comprehends the value of the vast resources of the land in terms of forests and wildlife. He befriends the local Native Americans and learns the Iroquois language.

1646 *(age 33, Peebles Island)*
In England, King Charles I is overthrown militarily amid deep divisions between the royalists and those favoring Parliament. The issue is about religious authority.

1647 *(age 34, Peebles Island)*
1. Pieter Stuyvesant begins a harsh reign as General Director of New Amsterdam. His position lasts seventeen years.
2. In his 1655 (or 1653?) book, A *Description of New Netherland*, Adriaen van der Donck writes of whales in the Hudson River as far north as Troy. He describes a whale that becomes stranded between the mouth of the Mohawk River and Cohoes Falls, a mile upriver. There it dies. The whale's decomposing carcass covers the water with a massive layer of oil and creates a terrible stench smelled kilometers away.
The first complete English edition was published in 2008, edited by Charles T. Gehring and William Starna, translated by Diederok W. Goedhuys, and introduced by Russell Shorto. (University of Nebraska Press).

1648 *(age 35, Peebles Island)*
The Treaty of Westphalia ends the wars between Spain and the Netherlands and all wars in Europe involving religious and

territorial conflicts. The Thirty Years' War in Europe is officially over.

1649 (age 36, Peebles Island)

The Parliament in London, led by Puritan Oliver Cromwell, convicts King Charles I of treason and executes him.

1655 (age 42, Peebles Island)

1. In the city of The Hague in the Dutch Republic, Christiaan Huygens, at age twenty-six, constructs a telescope. With it he observes the rings of Saturn and the moon, Titan, that orbits around the planet. A year later he invents the pendulum clock.

2. Jews, having earned the rights of settlement, come to New Amsterdam.

1660 (age 47, Peebles Island)

1. King Louis XIV of France declares that northern North America is a royal province. The promise of ample living space in the colonies induces large numbers of French citizens to emigrate.

2. King Charles II, son of Charles I, returns from exile in France under a triumphant welcoming by the English public grown weary of their dysfunctional Parliament.

3. Jacques Cortelyou, a cartographer from Utrecht, surveys the city of New Amsterdam and creates a map entitled "Picture of the City of Amsterdam in New Netherland." It becomes known as the Castello Plan of 1660. In Brooklyn today there is a street called Cortelyou Road. The cartographer's name also identifies a subway station stop, a branch of the Brooklyn Public Library, and an elementary school.

1662 *(age 49, Peebles Island)*
At a Jesuit missionary outpost among the Chippewas on the Ste.
Marie River (connecting Lake Superior and Lake Huron), the
French begin a campaign to claim the territory west of the Allegheny
Mountains. This territory would extend along the Mississippi River
to New Orleans.

1663 *(age 50, Peebles Island)*
The secretive "Invisible College," dedicated to the sciences, is
officially recognized by King Charles II. This group of scientists
now becomes known as The Royal Society of London for Improving
Natural Knowledge. The great scientific minds of the age are now
free to explore the physical and living world in the open. A Golden
Age of Discovery suddenly comes into being.

1664 *(age 51, Peebles Island)*
With English warships threatening the shores of New Amsterdam,
Pieter Stuyvesant cedes Dutch-held New Netherland without a
single blast of gun.(A stipulation in the 1667 Treaty of Breda to
end the Anglo-Dutch War, however, guarantees that the Dutch
would control naval trading routes and maintain their hold on
the global spice market. The truce agreement would also protect
certain Dutch rights; these will turn up a century later in the
Congressional Bill of Rights.) In 1664 King Charles II names his
younger brother James, Duke of York and Albany, sovereign of the
entire possession of New Netherland.

1665 *(age 52, Peebles Island)*
The Great Plague of London breaks out, killing at least one
hundred thousand residents. The bacteria causing bubonic plague
are carried by black rats that come into proximity with humans.

1666 *(age 53, Peebles Island)*

The Great Fire of London occurs, consuming eighty per cent of the city. Flames from a bakery on Pudding Lane are whipped by a strong east to west wind. Highly flammable medieval houses of wood, which use tar for caulking, stand no chance of survival.

1672 *(age 59, Peebles Island)*

On August 22nd in 1672, an eclipse occurs in New York State. It is the first and only total eclipse to cross the state in seven thousand years. The duration of totality is two minutes and fifteen seconds.

1675 *(age 62, Peebles Island)*

In eastern Massachusetts and Rhode Island, the Wampanoags protest the increasing domination by the English. The resulting uprising, King Philip's War, is a prolonged conflict with great numbers of deaths on both sides and a disaster for the Native Americans.

1681 *(age 68, Mt. Marcy. Retires to live alone alongside a stream.)*

After being rejected by the Massachusetts Bay Colony, the Quakers, under leadership of William Penn, obtain a charter from King Charles II for creating a community in Pennsylvania. The following year Penn proclaims that people of all faiths may practice their religion here with full tolerance, although only Protestants may hold office. He makes a pact promising peaceful relationships with the Leni Lenape (or Delawares).

1685 *(age 72, Mount Marcy)*

France declares the revocation of The Edict of Nantes. This means that religious tolerance is no longer permitted in the nation. Only Roman Catholicism is allowed.

1689 *(age 76, Mount Marcy)*
Scottish philosopher John Locke proposes that science, philosophy, and government should be entirely independent of religion. In 1776 this principle is adopted by the American Founding Fathers in their Declaration of Independence.

1692 *(age 79, Mount Marcy. Starts writing her Memoirs. Last entry, 28 Dec of this year.)*
In Salem, Massachusetts twenty people are accused of witchcraft and executed.

PART III

Assessment Suggestions

Note to the Teacher

Since the questions presented in this section refer to all five novels in the series, you will want to select only those questions that are relevant to your specific novel or lesson plan. Some questions are followed by answers, while others are intended to be open-ended and thought-provoking, generating perhaps some lively class discussions.

Matching Columns:
Names and Places

Tail Feather

1. "People of the Longhouse"
2. Tail Feather's canoe companion
3. Grandfather's nickname
4. Long-Distance runner
5. Tribe in southern river valley
6. Tribe trading with the Dutch
7. The River-That-Flows-Two-Ways
8. The Tall Girl
9. Tail Feather's pet wolf
10. Cloud-Splitter

A. Restless Wings
B. Kykoo
C. Mt. Marcy
D. BaBa
E. The Hudson
F. Kicking Elk
G. Mohicans
H. *Haudenosaunee*
I. The Healer
J. Lenape

Answers: 1. H, 2. F, 3. D, 4. A, 5. J, 6. G, 7. E, 8. I, 9. B, 10. C

Laughing Rain and Awakens Corn

1. Tail Feather's mother		A. Guiding Star
2. Tail Feather's father		B. Noisy Goose
3. Tail Feather's baby sister		C. Meadow-Bird Singing
4. Tail Feather's adventurous sister		D. The Three Sisters
5. Tail Feather's grandfather		E. Morning Blossom
6. Tail Feather's aunt		F. Kicking Elk
7. Mohawk Chief		G. Deganawidah
8. Laughing Rain's admirer		H. Sky Flower
9. The Peacemaker		I. Awakens Corn
10. Squash, corn, and beans		J. Red Sun

Answers: 1. E, 2. F, 3. H, 4. I, 5. A, 6. C, 7. J, 8. B, 9. G, 10. D

Sky Flower

1. Sky Flower's birthplace		A. Walsingham
2. Sky Flower's English name		B. Kinshasa
3. Invalid girl		C. Jacob
4. Tavern-keeper in New Amsterdam		D. Janneke
5. Kitchen maid		E. Harold
6. Puritan gardener		F. Lionel
7. Lord of the Manor		G. Van Hoevenberg
8. English actor		H. Gwendolyn
9. Faithful helper		I. Tahawus
10. Good student		J. Katrina

Answers: 1. I, 2. H., 3. J, 4. G, 5. B, 6. E, 7. A, 8. F, 9. C, 10. D

Johannes van der Zee

1. Seaport in Holland	A. Reginald
2. Cabin boy	B. Tahawus
3. Son of a Dutch merchant	C. Ingmar
4. Sailor from Copenhagen	D. Tail Feather
5. Captain of *The Unicorn*	E. Hoorn
6. Dutch trading post	F. Awakens Corn
7. River tribe supplying pelts	G. Johannes
8. Mohawk friend	H. Fort Nassau
9. Mohawk girl	I. Mohicans
10. Mohawk village	J. Vroom

Answers: 1. E, 2. A, 3. G, 4. C, 5. J, 6. H, 7. I, 8. D, 9. F, 10. B

Mary Walsingham

1. Mary's birthplace	A. Rebecca
2. Dutch trader	B. Littleton
3. Adams family poet	C. Veronica
4. Local Connecticut tribe	D. Jeremy
5. Mary's horse	E. Pieter
6. Caretaker of the Orangery	F. Podunks
7. Head of the Adams household	G. "Sir Francis Drake"
8. Puritan settlement	H. Harold
9. One of Mary's older sisters	I. Angel
10. The Walsingham cat	J. Hartford

Answers: 1. B, 2. E., 3. A, 4. F, 5. I, 6. H, 7. D, 8. J, 9. C, 10. G

Reading Comprehension

1. Pre-reading Word List

A pre-reading word list will provide students with a head start in understanding the key words in the story. It is a commonly used learning tool beneficial to all learners of English, native as well as non-native. Choose words that you think the students might not understand. Go over pronunciation as well as meanings and have the students use each word in an original sentence. Here are a few suggestions:

Tail Feather
a. palisades
b. longhouse
c. flint
d. wampum
e. cookfire

Laughing Rain and Awakens Corn

a. the elders

b. cradleboard

c. pact

d. missionary

e. shaman

Johannes van der Zee

a. sloop

b. scurvy

c. "the savages" or *de Wilden*

d. flintlocks

e. beaver pelts

Sky Flower

a. quill

b. bilge

c. bathhouse

d. orangery

e. eclipse

Mary Walsingham

a. muzzle

b. sidesaddle

c. blacksmith

d. Puritan

e. meetinghouse

2. Content Questions

Book 1, *Tail Feather*

1. What is one thing that makes Tail Feather different from the others in his village?

2. What is the first unwise decision that he makes?

3. Why does he want to go on the trading expedition with the clan elders?

4. What dangerous thing does he do while on top of the mountain?

5. Where does he hear about strange tales and monsters?

6. How does he prove that he is worthy of joining the expedition?

7. What is the Mohawk custom that precedes a long trip by tribal members?

8. What do Tail Feather's sisters make for him to take on his journey?

9. Who shares his canoe as a fellow paddler?

10. How do the Mohawks avoid detection by the Mohican Fire Dancers?

11. Why does Tail Feather want to see the home of the Angry-River-Spirit?

12. What does Kicking Elk reveal about his early life?

13. What does Tail Feather learn about the fishing practices of other tribes along the river?

14. What saves the Mohawks from the arrows of an enemy tribe?

15. Who takes care of Tail Feather when he becomes sick?

16. What amazing thing does Tail Feather see when he reaches a wide place in the river?

17. What is the object that the boy on the ship tosses to him?

18. In what ways are the island traders different from the Mohawks?

19. What is the creature called "Sea-Mountain-With-The-Tiny-Eye"?

20. How does Tail Feather feel as he is about to make the trip back home?

Book 1, Content Answers

1. He is left-handed.
2. He tries to follow Restless Wings, the Running Man, when he is unprepared to do so.
3. He wants to prove his worth and see the world.
4. He starts a fire that is spotted by an enemy tribe.
5. in the longhouse where the elders tell stories
6. He excels at all tasks and impresses the villagers with his diligence.
7. a cleansing ritual in the sweat lodge
8. a pair of leather moccasins lined with rabbit fur and tassels of deer hair. The one from Laughing Rain has blue porcupine quills while the one from Awakens Corn has red quills.
9. his father, Kicking Elk
10. At dark they move supplies overland and then paddle underneath the rocky ledge.
11. He is curious, and others in his tribe have never seen it before.
12. He was a Ramapough, captured and later accepted by the Mohawks as a member of their tribe.
13. They use nets to catch large fish swimming upriver.
14. A storm arises suddenly, and the enemy canoes capsize.
15. a Healer from the Shorakkopoch tribe. Tail Feather calls her "the tall girl."
16. a sailing ship
17. a blue hat
18. They are well-fed traders dressed in colorful clothing.
19. a whale
20. homesick, yet confident that he will have another great adventure

Book 2, *Laughing Rain and Awakens Corn*

1. Who are these girls?

2. What did weather conditions at the time of their birth have to do with the naming of the baby girls?

3. What are some of their tribal tasks?

4. Which girl is cautious and quiet?

5. Which girl is adventuresome and daring?

6. Why have the sisters felt such a special bond?

7. About what do the sisters disagree?

8. What kind of person is "Aunt Meadow-Bird-Singing"?

9. Why was she always critical of Morning Blossom in years past?

10. Why does Awakens Corn run away to the top of Cloud-Splitter?

11. What does she discover at the pond high up on the mountain?

12. How does her search for peace turn into days of disaster?

13. Who finds Awakens Corn and leads her back to Tahawus?

14. What is Chief Red Sun's advice?

15. Does the plan for an excursion around the lake end the sisters' quarrel?

16. What strange sight in the cornfield amazes the sisters?

17. How do most villagers react to the missionary's words?

18. Does Brother André Benoît show genuine interest in the lives of the Native peoples (Wyandots and Mohawks)?

19. Which family member does not return to Tahawus?

20. What is Laughing Rain's compromise as she tries to satisfy her sister's desire for adventure?

Book 2, Content Answers

1. Tail Feather's identical twin sisters
2. The needed rain ended the long drought and so, the "laughing" rain nourished or "awakened" the wilting corn.
3. planting seeds, preparing food for the winter, cleaning hides, gutting fish, deer, and other carcasses, keeping the cookfire going, making pots, baskets, and leather clothing
4. Laughing Rain
5. Awakens Corn
6. They are identical twins, which means they are physically completely alike.
7. the desire of Awakens Corn to visit far-away places
8. a no-nonsense person with no sense of humor
9. Her little sister never did her tasks correctly in the Mohawk way.
10. to think about why she is different from her sister who is satisfied with her life
11. a clear reflection of her face and a fly caught in a spider web
12. She gets lost, becomes drenched in the rain, breaks her arm, and is cold and hungry.
13. Kykoo, her brother's wolf (rhymes with Haiku or HIGH coo)
14. to forget quarrels and make peace instead
15. No.
16. a red-haired, white-faced person in black clothing
17. They are upset, thinking that the message is not in keeping with their own beliefs.
18. No.
19. Kicking Elk, the father
20. to have Awakens Corn show her the pond on Cloud-Splitter

Book 3, *Johannes van der Zee*

1. From what seaport does *The Unicorn* sail?

2. What does the figurehead on the ship represent?

3. What are two words that describe a sailor's shipboard duties?

4. Who is Reginald?

5. Why did Reginald's family move to Leyden in the Dutch Republic?

6. What foolish thing does Johannes do while high up on the bowsprit?

7. How does Ingmar, the sailor from Copenhagen, help Johannes?

8. What is the cargo that merchant Tuinstra hopes will be profitable one day?

9. What does the term "Dead Man's Breath" mean?

10. What does Pilot-Navigator Escobar do for Johannes?

11. How does Master Vroom deal with transgressions by the crew (talking back, fighting)?

12. What happens when *The Unicorn* reaches the trading post in New Netherland?

13. What does Master Vroom tell Joost, the fur trader?

14. What does Rut do to enrage the Mohicans?

15. What proves to Johannes that Tail Feather was the same *Wilde* he had seen three years earlier?

16. How do the two boys get to know one another?

17. What impression does Johannes have about the Mohawks in Tail Feather's village?

18. How does Johannes upset the tribal elders?

19. How is Fort Nassau, the trading post on Castle Island, destroyed?

20. What does Johannes think about as he prepares to return to Holland?

Book 3, Content Answers

1. Hoorn
2. a unicorn, a mythical animal suggesting a prosperous voyage for the ship owners and investors
3. dangerous and difficult
4. the cabin boy whom the sailors tease with the name "Tulip"
5. to be free to practice their religion
6. He leans over too far.
7. He grabs Johannes to safety and teaches him how to make secure knots.
8. tulips
9. the time when the sea is calm and a ship is unable to move
10. He lets him use the navigational instrument called a cross-staff.
11. He is cruel, demanding extremely harsh punishments.
12. Dutch goods for trading are off-loaded, while beaver pelts are on-loaded.
13. to remain at the post until Spring
14. He kills one of them with a long object that makes a loud noise.
15. T. F. returns the original blue hat sewn with the Dutch sailor's initials, JvdZ.
16. They meet at a clearing in the forest and exchange words and ideas.
17. They are hard-working and interested in his world across the ocean.
18. He is attracted to Awakens Corn, thereby endangering tribal values about race and culture.
19. It is washed away in a spring flood.
20. his earlier prejudices about native people and his real interests and talents

Book 4, *Sky Flower*

1. Why is Sky Flower, as a little girl, often given easy chores to do in the shade?

2. Why does Chief Red Sun allow Sky Flower to leave their village?

3. What is Sky Flower supposed to do in the home of the Dutch trader?

4. How does she learn how to count and read in Dutch?

5. What disease leaves pock marks or scars on her face?

6. What kind of work does she do in New Amsterdam?

7. How does she start to learn English?

8. How does she help Mary?

9. What does her stay at the Manor House teach her about English people?

10. Who is Kinshasa?

11. About what does Harold warn Sky Flower?

12. How does Harold explain the execution scene that Sky Flower witnessed?

13. What happens in Newcastle-upon-Tyne?

14. What does Sky Flower see that inspires her to leave England?

15. How does she get to the port city of Plymouth?

16. Who is Eunice and what does she tell Sky Flower?

17. Why does Sky Flower not rejoin her siblings and their families in the mountains?

18. Who is Pieter, the man who helped her build a schoolhouse?

19. Of all her students, which one shares Sky Flower's love for the earth and all its creatures?

20. How does Meadow-Bird-Singing change in terms of personality and outlook?

Book 4, Content Answers

1. Her skin is sun-sensitive, and it blisters easily.
2. She has difficulty accepting clan duties and many elders consider her lazy.
3. care for his sick daughter
4. She helps Katrina with her schoolwork.
5. smallpox
6. She serves food and drinks to customers and helps with chores in the tavern.
7. by speaking with English customers in the tavern and later with the young prisoner, Bertrand, during the voyage to England
8. She discovers Mary's deafness and shows her how to communicate with hand signs.
9. They are either hard-working servants or non-working privileged people.
10. She is a young kitchen servant who shares attic sleeping quarters with Sky Flower. As a young child she arrived in England on a slave ship from Africa.
11. He warns about the evil practices advocated by the Church of England and the Roman Catholic Church, and by all actors, including Lionel, Sky Flower's new friend.
12. The peasants were hanged presumably because they stole food or hunted illegally on a noble's estate.
13. Not finding Lionel there as he promised, heartbroken Sky Flower tries to drown herself.
14. "Grandmother Moon" who reminds Sky Flower of her Mohawk culture
15. She walks from northern England to the Devon coastline in the south.

16. a Puritan woman in Boston who tells her about a Norwegian ship about to sail to New Amsterdam
17. Having experienced both Dutch and English cultures, Sky Flower now feels like an outsider among her own people.
18. He is the brother of the sick girl whom Sky Flower had helped in Fort Orange.
19. Janneke
20. Her new purpose in life is to maintain tribal traditions. At the same time, she becomes kinder and less severe in her dealings with others.

Book 5, *Mary Walsingham*

1. Why is Mary, as a child, considered badly-behaved?

2. How does Sky Flower learn that Mary is deaf?

3. Who becomes the child's friend and teacher?

4. What special talents does Mary have?

5. Why does Mary name her foal Angel?

6. How does Mary react as the blacksmith strikes the hammer on the anvil?

7. Although her parents allow her to work in the stables, how do they want her to dress?

8. Why does Lord Walsingham dismiss the famous trainer?

9. What are Mary's tasks during the sea voyage?

10. Who is Jeremy Adams?

11. Why does Lord Walsingham send his letter to Boston?

12. How does Mary adjust to life in a Puritan home?

13. What is "The House of Good Hope"?

14. What does Mary notice about the clothing of the Dutch sailors?

15. How does Pieter entertain the children while the trading is going on?

16. How does Mary help Rebecca?

17. How does Mary help Thomas, Rebecca's shy brother?

18. What does Mary do to earn the disapproval of the Adams family?

19. How does Mistress Adams help Mary recover from the loss of Angel?

20. What is Pieter's connection to Sky Flower?

Book 5, Content Answers

1. She does not follow instructions and she does not speak.
2. The cat knocks over a vase, causing a loud noise; everyone but Mary reacts.
3. Sky Flower
4. drawing and interacting with animals
5. The white patch on the forehead looks like an angel with wings.
6. She feels a vibration, or a quivering caused by the heavy pounding.
7. in proper clothing that befits her social status
8. He realizes that his daughter's well-being is more important than a perfectly trained horse.
9. calming and feeding the animals and cleaning up after them
10. the Puritan buyer of her father's horses
11. He does not know that the Adams family has resettled in Connecticut.
12. She joins in gratefully and completes her chores willingly.
13. It is a Dutch fort and trading post near the English settlement of Hartford.
14. It is very colorful, unlike the drab colors worn by the Puritans.
15. He puts on an amusing puppet show using his hands and a stocking. At another time he juggles three clay balls in ongoing rotation.
16. She suggests a solution for easing and even preventing Rebecca's recurring migraine headaches. Her ideas put an end to the rising suspicion among the neighbors that the girl may be a witch.

17. She shows an interest in his treasures and urges Rebecca to reach out to him more often.
18. Without a chaperone and without letting the Adams family know of her plans, she spends a day with Pieter in the countryside.
19. She comforts Mary as she sits beside her bed at night.
20. Sky Flower was his sister Katrina's caretaker in Fort Orange and, years later, the teacher for whom he helped build a schoolhouse.

C.

Critical Thinking

For class discussions: Answers will vary.

Book 1, *Tail Feather*

1. If you wanted to become a long-distance runner, like the Running Man, what would you need to do?

2. Since there were no formal schools as we know them today, how do you think the Mohawk children learned about their history and culture?

3. What is the lesson about Nature that Chapter 11, "Blue Ledges," teaches? (Blue Ledges is a natural site along the upper Hudson River.)

4. What explains the relative silence of the Mohawk paddlers after seeing the Dutch ship?

Book 2, *Laughing Rain and Awakens Corn*

1. If you could give advice to Laughing Rain and Awakens Corn about their big disagreement, what would you say to them?

2. Why do you suppose that Morning Blossom understands Awakens Corn's desires better than Laughing Rain does?

3. What explains Chief Red Sun's permission for Noisy Goose and his friends to go hunting in enemy territory?

Book 3, *Johannes van der Zee*

1. If you worked on *The Unicorn* as a sailor, what would your day be like?

2. Why do think that Master Vroom would take the time talk to Johannes, an ordinary Seaman, about his desire to become a ship's captain?

3. If you were a member of the crew left to spend the winter at Fort Nassau, what would be your biggest concern and why?

4. Why does Johannes keep thinking that the *Wilden* (pronounced *VIL-den*) are always trying to do him harm?

5. As you look at Johannes's behavior throughout the story, do you notice any changes in his ideas and viewpoints?

Book 4, *Sky Flower*

1. By what clever way does Sky Flower obtain passage on the *Prins van Oranje,* the ship sailing from Beverwyck to New Amsterdam?

2. Sky Flower once said no one person had ever asked her about her own religious beliefs: not the van Stroomers, not the Walsinghams, not Harold, and not Lionel. What does this fact say about the European view of Native American spirituality?

3. What, other than homesickness, would make Sky Flower want to leave "civilized" England and return to the forest?

4. In Boston: Why does Sky Flower see herself as a "mixed-up longhouse"?

5. What does the arrival of Europeans mean for the Indigenous nations of North America?

Book 5, *Mary Walsingham*

1. Even though, as boys, Lord Walsingham and Master Adams both enjoyed an upper-class education, as adults they have different views of a person's place in society. How do their religions influence their views of social class?

2. In view of the hardships ahead, why do you think the Walsinghams finally permitted their daughter to make the journey overseas?

3. How does the attitude of Mary's mother toward her daughter change over the years?

4. After looking through her book, *Countrey Contentments or the English Huswife,* Mary feels empowered. What does she now realize?

5. What do Mary's accomplishments say about her as a person?

D.

Traditional Prejudices

For class discussions: What traditional belief or prejudice explains the behavior cited in each book below?

Book 2 Iroquois-Mohawk prejudices: Tail Feather and his family are upset because Johannes and Awakens Corn appear to like each other very much. Why?

Book 3 Dutch prejudices: When Johannes tries to explain that Tail Feather is not an enemy, Rut gets angry at him. Why?

Book 4 Dutch prejudices: Katrina's parents do not want her to teach Sky Flower how to write. Why? English prejudices: The Walsinghams never want to look closely into the reasons for their daughter's unruly behavior. Why?

Book 5 English prejudices: Lord and Lady Walsingham do not thank Sky Flower, the servant they call "Gwendolyn," after she helps their daughter learn to communicate. Why?

E.

Spirituality and Behavior

For class discussions: How do religious or spiritual beliefs affect the actions and conduct of: ...?

- Tail Feather's family (Books 1, 2)
- Reginald's family (Book 3)
- The Walsingham family (Book 4)
- The Adams family (Book 5)

Native American Aspects

Many different Indigenous groups are mentioned throughout The River Quintet series: the **Iroquois** bands and clans of the Seneca, Cayuga, Onondaga, Oneida, Mohawk, and Wyandot/Wendat (Huron) nations in Books 1, 2, 3, and 4, and several **Algonquin** groups including the Mohicans, Lenapes (Munsees, Wappingers, Ramapough-Lenapes, Shorakkopochs, and Canarsees) and Mi'kmaq in Books 1, 2 and 3; the Powhatans, Wampanoags, and Narragansetts in Book 4, and finally the Podunks in Book 5.

Suggested answers are offered, but students should be encouraged to add their own ideas or comments.

Book 1, *Tail Feather*, F.

1. What kind of lessons do the night stories told to Iroquois-Mohawk children contain?

2. What is the purpose of the game "Little Brother of War"?

3.   The woodland tribes depend on light-weight canoes made of birch wood. What kind of canoes do the Canarsees and other islanders use and why?

4.   How does the Shorakkapoch shaman help Tail Feather?

5.   Where is the sacred burial ground of the island people, and how does the funeral procession get there?

6.   According to Iroquois/Mohawk beliefs, is there a happy and peaceful place after death for good tribal members who held strong to traditional values?

Book 1, F. Suggested Answers

1.   lessons that contain the values and beliefs of the tribe
2.   to prepare young boys for real warfare
3.   dug-out canoes of heavy wood to carry large loads and withstand ocean waves
4.   He performs a traditional ritual of incantations and dancing to draw away the bad spirits of illness. His helper, "the tall girl," eases Johannes's fever with cool compresses and offers him nourishment as the fever lessens.
5.   high up on the cliffs across the river to the west. Today this area is called the Palisades because the cliffs look like tall structures fortified with timber. The islanders, carrying their deceased member, cross the river in boats.
6.   Yes.

Book 2, *Laughing Rain and Awakens Corn*, F.

1. 1. What does Guiding Star say about wild animals and why should his granddaughters not be upset about Kykoo's disappearance?

2. Based on Guiding Star's long life and his dying words to his family, explain the Iroquois view of life and death.

3. Chief Red Sun tells the twins how peace came to the Iroquois when the tribes finally agreed to stop quarreling with one another. By what name do we know this agreement which unified five different family tribes? Why does he tell this story instead of punishing Awakens Corn for running away?

Book 2, F. Suggested Answers

1. It is normal for a domesticated animal like the wolf, Kykoo, to yearn for its natural wild environment. Occasional disappearances are to be expected.

2. It is only natural that a person who is born will eventually die. That person is expected to pass along tribal values and life's lessons to a younger one, who, in turn will repeat the cycle. Death is just a transition and a hand-over of wisdom and lore. The deceased one will rest in a peaceful and happy realm. No one should mourn, at least, not for long.

3. the Iroquois Confederacy. He wants the girls to follow suit: to understand their different viewpoints and to have a good relationship with each other.

Book 3, *Johannes van der Zee*, F.

1. Curiosity is a natural human trait. What does a Mohican do, perhaps out of curiosity, that enrages Rut, one of the Dutch sailors left at Fort Nassau?

2. What does the Mohican village look like in contrast to the Mohawk palisaded village of Tahawus?

3. How do members of this river tribe help Johannes and Tail Feather after the trading post is washed away?

4. How does Gentle-Rain-Falling help Johannes?

5. A sense of humor is another natural human trait. How does Tail Feather show Johannes that he, too, has a sense of humor?

Book 3, F. Suggested Answers

1. He goes into the trading post and picks up a pewter plate. Rut thinks that the *Wilde* is going to steal it.
2. Palisaded timber does not encircle the village. The houses are mostly round with cone-style peaks or domed roofs. The longhouses are small by Mohawk standards.
3. They allow the boys to stay for several days and repair the hole in their canoe.
4. To lessen the pain of itching caused by poison ivy, she applies a soothing paste to his blistered skin.
5. He plays a joke on Johannes by suggesting an impossible tracking test.

Book 4, *Sky Flower*, F

1. "Princess" Pocahontas, dressed in a lovely gown, is paraded through London as an exotic specimen from a faraway land. What is the name of her nation and where is it located?

2. While in Boston, Sky Flower talks with a Narragansett Running Man who carries a sash of wampum over a shoulder. What is his purpose and where is he going?

3. What does Meadow-Bird-Singing say about Noisy Goose?

Book 4, F. Suggested Answers
1. **Powhatan, from the area we now call Virginia**
2. **to take a message "written" in shells to the Boston Wampanoags**
3. **He becomes addicted to alcohol and loses all sense of Mohawk values and obligations.**

Book 5, *Mary Walsingham*

1. What can you say about the Podunks? Consider their presence at the trading sessions in Hartford and their hospitality to Mary.

2. As Mary is riding her horse one day, four members of an unknown tribe come upon her, pointing arrows. What happens when one of them opens her travel bag and discovers its contents, and then how do they all react to Mary's grand show of defiance?

Book 5, F. Suggested Answers

1. They adjust to the presence of English settlers in their territory and are content to trade goods with the Dutch. Economic interests help maintain peace for all. Knowing Mary from earlier visits to Hartford makes them eager to help her when she arrives in their village lost and wet. They offer her dry clothes, a place to sleep and food.

2. The rider who opens her bag finds things that are unfamiliar and smelly: bread and cheese. He does not like the odor. When another man touches Angel's forehead, Mary amazes them all with a sharp slap on his hand and angry gestures that mean: "Don't mess with me!" They decide to leave her alone. They are stunned at the strange food and the unexpected behavior of a white woman.

Examining Viewpoints

1. It is often said that people all over the world and from different ethnic and religious beliefs have basically the same goals and desires for health and happiness. Would you agree?

2. What might you have in common with Tail Feather: do you understand his desire to be taken seriously by adults? Can you understand his frustrations when he "goofs up" and does foolish things? Are these feelings universal in all young people, do you think?

3. Can you understand the desire of Awakens Corn to do something different? Is wanting to see what lies beyond one's own turf always a terrible thing? Is she, a Mohawk girl, any less likely to want to travel as a person of another ethnicity or time?

4. As Johannes leaves Holland, he upholds the traditional values and viewpoints of other Dutch people. Events on the ship, at Fort Nassau and at Tahawus (Tail Feather's village) make him reevaluate his viewpoints concerning his own people and the

Wilden. Can you explain that change and do you think it was a logical conclusion? Or if not, what would have liked him to say or do?

5. During her long stay at the manor house Sky Flower learns about class distinctions in English society. What specifically does she not understand? Was she able to make the Walsinghams and Harold understand her Iroquois-Mohawk values? As you read the story, did you hope that Sky Flower would become more "English," or did you want her to stay Mohawk at heart?

6. What do social class and privilege have to do with the Walsinghams' view of their badly behaved child? Are they afraid of what the neighbors might say? Do you agree that "imperfections" are something to hide?

7. Why do Lord and Lady Walsingham believe the doctor instead of Mary? He examines Mary's hearing only once, whereas Sky Flower has witnessed the proof of the child's deafness.

H.

Memorable Scenes

1. Choose a scene from the book you read. Describe:
- what the scene is about.
- what makes it special for you.
- what your reactions were as you read it.

Scenes from *Tail Feather* (Book 1)

1. TF sending smoke signals on top of Cloud-Splitter
2. Blue Ledges showing the harmony of nature
3. TF and his fellow travelers avoiding capture by the Fire Dancers

Scenes from *Laughing Rain and Awakens Corn* (Book 2)

1. AC and LR seeing a red-headed stranger in the cornfield
2. AC finding refuge in a cave with a snake
3. AC and LR being comforted by their grandfather, Guiding Star

Scenes from *Johannes van der Zee* (Book 3)

1. Reginald being told that he must climb to the top of the mast
2. Johannes itching from poison ivy and smelling like a skunk
3. Johannes remembering his "nightmare of numbers"

Scenes from *Sky Flower* (Book 4)

1. SF observing the other passengers during the carriage ride to the Manor House
2. SF being interviewed by Lady Walsingham in the "great room"
3. SF describing Raphael, the dance instructor

Scenes from *Mary Walsingham* (Book 5)

1. Mary reacting to Arthur's attempts at training Angel
2. Mary carrying out her tasks in the bilge (or bottom) of the ship
3. Mary observing the Puritans as they listen to a sermon at the meetinghouse

2. Did you enjoy another scene, one not listed here? If so, give a brief description of what it was about, and why you liked it. In which book of the series is it found?

I.

Literary Evaluations

Answers will vary.

1. Which book of the series did you read (title and subtitle)?

2. What is the author's name?

3. Did you like the main character?

4. What events helped form the main character's vision for the future?

5. What part of the story did you like best and why?

6. What part of the story did you like least and why?

7. What general aspects of the story interested you? (setting, issues, plot, characters)

8. Who was the narrator, (the person who told the story)?

9. Which secondary characters appealed to you?

10. What is the "take-away" of this reading for you personally?

11. Did you look something up in the Reference Notes (Books 1,
    2, 3, and 5) or Overview/Timeline (Book 4)? if yes, what?

12. Did the book inspire you to learn more about a particular
    subject? if yes, what?

PART IV

Projects and Class Activities

Selection of Activities

1. **One novel of your choice!** Choose a book (1, 2, 3, 4, or 5)

- Imagine another ending. **Write** another version of the final moments or **tell** the class about how you would change the ending.

- **Draw** and **label** a picture showing five things (such as animals and buildings) that stand out as principal elements in the story. Draw a picture of the main character, as well, and list adjectives that describe that person.

- Using your own words, **tell** the story to your class. Mention the geographical setting and the names of the main characters. Give highlights of major events in the plot.

2. All the Novels: The River Quintet Series

- **Draw four pictures depicting the names** Tail Feather, Laughing Rain, Awakens Corn, and Sky Flower. Under each picture write a brief explanation of how each baby received this name.

- **Make a map of New Netherland,** including the trading post called Fort Nassau and the villages of New Amsterdam, Fort Orange (later expanded and renamed Beverwyck), and Hartford. Show the two rivers associated with them and identify them by their Dutch and English names.

- **Make a chart or picture to show the spiritual paths** that guided the lives of the following groups: Tail Feather and his family, the Walsingham family, and the Adams family. Use symbols such as a plant, a stained-glass window, and a Bible to represent the beliefs of the Native American animists, the members of the Church of England and the sect called Puritans. Add additional symbols for each group.

- **Make a storyboard** with five sections, one for each of the five novels. Select clip art or other pictures that represent major events in each book. Use these pictures to talk about each story.

3. The Novels Individually

Book 1: *Tail Feather*
- **Sketch a Mohawk village** showing palisades, longhouses, and a meeting post. Include items important to the inhabitants, such as flint, arrowheads, deerskins, bearskins, snowshoes, bows and arrows, squash, beans and corn, baskets woven from reeds and other plants, a headdress with antlers, and a robe decorated with turkey feathers.

- **Build an overnight shelter in the form of a lean-to.** Model yours after Tail Feather's shelter of twigs, branches, leaves, moss, and pine needles. If done outside, photograph your lean-to and show your photo to the class.

- **Show others how to make a canoe.** List the step-by step instructions given by Tail Feather's grandfather, and then draw a large picture of a canoe with paddles and filled with travel items for the journey.

- **Make a poster showing food for the journey:** Write out and/or show pictures of the ingredients used to make journey cakes. Write or show by a drawing what the Mohawks did to soften them once they became stale and hard. Show other foods that the paddlers ate during their river journey. Make a drawing showing a person drinking fresh water but not drinking salt water. Show foods that the islanders shared with their visitors.

Book 2: *Laughing Rain and Awakens Corn*

- On a large poster board **show the importance of the deer** to the Native Americans. What parts of the deer did they find useful? What things did they make out of these parts? Explain specifically how two of these items were made, and who had the main responsibility for doing this work.

- **Make a pair of moccasins.** Improvise by getting pieces of felt or imitation leather, and cutting outlines of each foot, making additional sections for the sides and the "vamps" (the area over the top of the toes). Connect them by sewing the parts together. Or follow specific directions in one of the online "how to" guides for making your own moccasins. You may wish to decorate them with beads or tassels.

Book 3: *Johannes van der Zee*

- **Make a map showing the oceanic voyage** of *The Unicorn* from Hoorn to the North River.

- **Tie a bowline knot** (pronounced BOH'-lin), one of the sailor's most useful knots. Reread the passage in Book 3 and/or choose an online instruction guide with a diagram. Show the class how to make it.

- **Make a replica of the orange, white and blue flag** of The Dutch Republic of the Seven United Netherlands. Use colored paper or pieces of felt, glue, and a yardstick for a mast.

Book 4: *Sky Flower*

- **Make a collage of pictures representing the Dutch settlement of *Beverwijck*.** Suggestions: wooden clogs, three-masted ships, beaver pelts, cows, milk and cheese, small houses with steep roofs, a blacksmith, a baker, a wheelwright, a one-room schoolhouse, a church, blue and white tiles, and *Sinterklaas* (or *Sint-Nicolaas*) and his Feast Day of Dec. 6.

- **Make a chart showing the ways the English people worked and played** in the early 17th century: draw pictures or use clipart to show the kinds of work laborers on the Walsingham estate and the townspeople performed. In addition, show the kinds of recreation they enjoyed at local festivals and on saints' days. Show types of upper-class recreation, as well.

- **Do a virtual tour of or take a field trip to Peebles Island**, (Cohoes, NY), the present-day site of Sky Flower's schoolhouse. Find out how the old 19th century factory buildings have been "repurposed," that is, how they are being used currently.

Book 5: *Mary Walsingham*

- **Make a chart showing animals important** to both the Native Americans and the English. Show how these animals were valued and/or for what purposes they were raised. Consider the animals owned by the wealthy Anglicans as well as by the Puritans. Draw or cut out pictures of these animals.

- **Try to express your thoughts** using hand signals or gestures, or search online for "how to sign" using American Sign Language videos. See if you can express one or two of the following messages:

  1. I have a boat.
  2. Do you like horses?
  3. Yes/No.

  Answers:

I	have	(a) boat.
Point to yourself.	Point hands to chest several times.	Clasp hands together with thumbs up.

(Do) you	like	like
Point to the person you are asking.	With fingers stretched out, put hand on your chest, then bring middle finger and thumb together.	Extend hand outward, away from you, while keeping the O shape intact. Smile to show enjoyment.

horses?	Yes	No
With each hand make an L-shape with thumb, middle and index fingers. Fold other fingers down. Put thumbs on temples and wiggle middle and index fingers up and down.	Make a closed fist, placing your thumb horizontally at base of the other four fingers. Move fist up and down, as if nodding. Smile to express affirmation.	Extend all fingers. Tuck ring and pinkie fingers under so that they touch palm. Bring down middle and pointer fingers to touch thumb. Extend hand outward, away from body. Frown to express negativity.

PART V

Resources for Further Study

Chart: Facts and Fiction

Facts	Fiction
1613 Adriaen Block explores the New Netherland area in his ship, the *Tijger*.	**1613** Tail Feather sees Block's ship as it sails up the *Noordrivier* ("North River"). He encounters Johannes, the cabin boy, while his sisters at home come face to face with a Jesuit missionary. His youngest sister, Sky Flower is born.
1614 After Block's ship is destroyed by fire, he spends the winter on "Manhattan Island." He builds the *Onrust,* finds the mouth of the CT River, and discovers *Block Eylandt* and *Roodt* (red) *Eylandt,* ("Rhode Island"), named for its red soil.	
1614-15 Construction of Fort Nassau, a fur trading post on Castle Island, just south of present-day Albany, NY.	

Facts	Fiction
	1616 Dutch sailor Johannes van der Zee, arrives at Fort Nassau. He becomes re-acquainted with Tail Feather who invites him to visit his Mohawk village. Johannes and Awakens Corn are attracted to one another. She now wants to travel and see new places. Her sister opposes this idea, as it would put the Iroquois heritage at risk.
1617 A flood caused by the spring thaw of river ice destroys Fort Nassau. Another fort is built on the confluence of the Normanskill and the North River but in 1618 it, too, is destroyed by a flood.	
1621 Eleven enslaved African men are brought to New Amsterdam to work for the Dutch West India Company.	**1621** Mary Walsingham of Littleton, England is born to an upper-class family of noble lineage.
1623-4 Construction of Fort Orange	
	1627 Willem and Liesbeth van Stroomer and their children settle in Fort Orange.
	1628 Sky Flower cares for their sick daughter, Katrina, then moves to New Amsterdam where she works as a tavern maid.

Facts	Fiction
1629-30 The Patroon system starts. Kilian van Rensselaer buys land on both sides of the river.	**1629** Sky Flower accepts a job offer to work as a servant in a manor house in England. She sails to London.
1630 The first large group of Dutch families (tradespeople and farmers) arrives at Fort Orange, and a small community outside its walls is established.	**1630** Sky Flower begins new duties as a governess to the Walsingham children. She is given the name Gwendolyn.
1636 Reverend Thomas Hooker establishes a Puritan community in Hartford (Connecticut).	
	1637 Sky Flower, (age 24), leaves England, visits her family in the mountains, and moves to a small island just north of *Beverwijck*.
	1639 Mary, 18, travels to Hartford, resides with the Adams family, and meets Pieter, the Dutch trader.
1640s The expanding community outside of Fort Orange gradually becomes known as *Beverwijck* or Beverwyck (Beaver Village or Beaver Town).	
1642-51 English Civil War	
1648 The first Dutch school is built in *Beverwijck*.	

Facts	Fiction
1692 Witch trials are held in Salem, Massachusetts	**1692** Sky Flower, (age 79) writes her memoirs from her mountain home. She dies presumably in December of this year.

Website Links and Suggested Reading

This section has four parts: ***Native Americans***, ***Cultural Centers and Museums***, ***Student Resources***, and ***Suggested Reading***. The links for the first part identify the contemporary presence of many Indigenous groups cited in The River Quintet series. Other links offer only information about a tribe or a topic, such as the New Netherland Colony or Deafness.

Native Americans

Iroquois Cited in The River Quintet

New York State
The *Haudenosaunee* Confederacy (called Iroquois Confederacy by the French and The League of Five Nations by the British), was formed in 1570. The Tuscaroras joined in 1722. The Iroquois are called the **"People of the Long House."** Website features

include the clan system, symbols, ceremonies, values, languages, common misconceptions, notable people, trade history, medicine, storytelling, and more.
See: https://www.haudenosauneeconfederacy.com

The Mohawk Nation or "People of the Flint" and "Keepers of the Eastern Door." The reservation of the Saint Regis Mohawk Tribe is in Akwesasne, New York. The nation's original home was in the Mohawk Valley of New York State. Website features include history and culture, as well as community issues. The reservation runs a casino and a resort hotel.
See: https://www.srmt-nsn.gov

The *Kanatsiohareke* Mohawk Community: located along the Mohawk River near Fonda, New York; founded by renowned Mohawk Elder, spiritual leader and award-winning educator, **Thomas R. Porter.** His community strives to retain traditional Mohawk values, and, additionally, to promote peace and understanding among all peoples. Website features include Mohawk culture, language immersion, annual festival, and newsletter.
See: http://www.mohawkcommunity.com

The Oneida Indian Nation, federally recognized, has a reservation near Oneida in central New York State. The Oneidas are called **"People of the Standing Stone."** Website features include a historical timeline of tribal events, a cultural center, and a language preservation program. It operates three casinos and oversees a large community.
See: https://www.oneidaindiannation.com

The Oneida Nation of Wisconsin, federally recognized, resides on a reservation created in 1838 for Oneidas expelled from their land in New York State. Website features include history and culture (including interactive games for language learning), as well as community issues.
See: https://www.oneida-nsn.gov

The Onondaga Nation, "People of the Hills" and "Keepers of the Central Fire." Members now reside in their ancestral homeland south of Syracuse, NY. They maintain traditional values and abstain from the sale of alcohol and all forms of gambling. Website features include a timeline, culture, land rights, current news, and videos.
See: https://www.onondaganation.org

The Cayuga Nation, "People of the Great Swamp," lived originally around Cayuga Lake in New York State. Website features include culture and tribal history relating to their involvement in the Revolutionary War and their subsequent forced removal to Buffalo Creek with the Senecas, to Ohio and to Ontario, Canada
See: https://cayuganation-nsn.gov

The Seneca Nation of Indians, "People of the Great Hill" and "Keepers of the Western Door": originally from the Finger Lakes region of central New York and the Genesee Valley of western New York. The Nation has three federally recognized reservations, Allegany, Cattaraugus, and Oil Springs, five territories and three casinos. Website features include history and culture, language promotion and community events.
See: https://sni.org

The Tonawanda Band of Senecas, a federally recognized tribe just east of the city of Buffalo, NY. Website features include the history of its separation from The Seneca Nation of Indians due to the sale of land at Buffalo Creek.
See: https://tonawandareservationhistoricalsociety.wordpress.com

Not cited in TRQ yet relevant: **The Tuscarora Nation or "People of the Shirt" or "Shirt-Wearing People."** Events: Early move of this Iroquois nation from New York to the Carolinas; defeat by colonial forces in the Tuscarora War (1711-1715); resettlement of some in New York State by those who joined the Haudenosaunee Confederacy in 1722, and of others who went to Ontario, Canada. The New York reservation is in Niagara County.
Contact through: https://bia.gov
For those resettled in Canada see: https://www.sixnations.ca
Many Tuscaroras remained in the south.
See: https://tuscaroranationnc.com

Ohio, Oklahoma, Michigan, Kansas, USA and Québec, Canada:
The Seneca-Cayugas of Ohio. The website outlines the history of former New York State bands seeking a place to live. Major events from 1750 to 1937.
See: https://ohiohistorycentral.org

The Seneca-Cayuga Nation of Oklahoma. Its website menu under "heritage," then "history" cites guides to each of these groups in the state. The community offerings include a cultural summer camp for young people.
See: https://sctribe.com (This nation is one of the thirty-nine Sovereign Tribal Nations in Oklahoma.)

The Wendat Confederacy. The Wyandots, (whose tribal name is **Wendat or Ouendat meaning "Island Dwellers or Peninsula People,"**) first lived along the St. Lawrence River and later settled on the northern shore of Lake Ontario and around the Georgian Bay. The French called them Hurons. With other tribes they formed a confederacy. Today's confederacy consists of the:

- **Huron-Wendat First Nation** of Wendake, Quebec, Canada.
  See: https://wendake.ca
- **Wyandot Nation of Anderdon** in Michigan.
  See https://www.wyandotofanderdon.com
- **Wyandot Nation of Kansas,**
  See: https://www.wyandot.org and the
- **Wyandotte Nation** in Oklahoma.
  See: https://wyandotte-nation.org

Algonquins Cited in The River Quintet

Central and southern N.Y.S. south to Delaware and points west
Lenape/Delaware: "The Original People or The Grandfathers."
Many displaced Lenape members went to Wisconsin, others to Ontario, Canada, and the most to Oklahoma. Several remained in the east.

Mohicans: The Stockbridge-Munsee Community Band of Mohican Indians or "People of the Waters that Are Never Still": a federally recognized nation in Wisconsin. Website features include their history, association with the Munsees, forced removal to Wisconsin, and Mohican and Munsee language lessons.
See: https://www.mohican.com

The Delawares in Oklahoma: The Delaware Nation Lenni Lenape, a federally recognized tribe referred to as the Delawares of Western Oklahoma. The Nation promotes the preservation of Lenape eastern woodlands culture and fluency in the language. It also oversees ancestral properties in eighteen other states. See: https://www.delawarenation-nsn.gov/history. Also: **The Delaware Tribe of Indians,** another federally recognized tribe referred to as the Eastern or Cherokee Delaware. Website features include efforts to preserve archaeological artifacts and heritage. See: https://delawaretribe.org

The Lenni-Lenape Nation of Pennsylvania: Website features include the treaty of Chief Tamanend and William Penn, the cultural center today, and contemporary events. See: https://www.lenape-nation.org

The Ramapough-Lenape Indian Nation, "Keepers of the Pass:" a Connecticut band that fled the Dutch and the English in the 17th century and settled in the mountains of present-day southeastern NY and northern NJ. The Nation is recognized by the state of New Jersey as a Native tribe. Website features include a "Ramapough Timeline," (mentioning, as well, the existence of the **Wappingers** between 1689 and 1696), a cultural center, and the "Munsee Three Sisters Farm."
See Ramapo Munsee Lenape Network at: https://ramapomunsee.net
See also "Ramapough Munsee History" at the Ramapough Culture and Land Foundation: https://ramapough.org

The Shorakkopochs or "People of the Wading Place": a Lenape (Delaware) tribe that once lived at the north end of Manhattan Island where the East River enters the Hudson River. Today a large

boulder is a reminder of the presence of this tribe. **Four links:**
1. a photo of **"Shorakkopoch Rock at Inwood Hill Park."**
According to the accompanying story, the "purchase" of Manhattan
by Peter Minuit from the Canarsees occurred underneath a tulip
tree in this northern section of the island. See: https://www.
atlasobscura.com/places/shorakkopoch. **2.** Many historians
believe that a site in Lower Manhattan was more likely the place of
this "purchase." PDF: "Where Did the Manhattan 'Purchase' Take
Place?" by Peter Douglas at https://www.newnetherlandinstitute.
org/download). **3.** Another site links the tribe's name to its
location, (a wading or low area between the ridges) and identifies
its settlement near the inlet into which Henry Hudson sailed in
1609. Search: Shorakkopoch Rock's Erratic Past at https://www.
geocaching.com/geocache/GC2RWJ1. **4.** Historical Marker Data-
base with facts and photo. Search: Tulip Tree Monument.
See: https://www.hmdb.org

The **Canarsees-(Canarsies), "People in a Fenced-in Place":**
a Munsee-speaking Lenape tribe formerly of western Long
Island and the New York metropolitan area. The link contains a
collection of resources pertaining to various local Lenape groups
and the Algonquian-speaking Shinnecock Nation in eastern Long
Island. Included: magazine and newsletter articles, maps, photos,
and a document by the N.Y.S. Education Department outlining
Indigenous teaching topics and resources.
See https://aich.org/mannahatta-fund-newsletter

Northern New England and Maritime Provinces of Canada
**The Wabanaki or "Dawnland" Confederacy: "The People of the
Dawn" or "People of the Land of the Rising Sun":** Five member

nations: Mi'kmaq / Micmac and Abenaki, (both cited in The River Quintet) and Penobscot, Maliseet, and Passamaquoddy.

The **Aroostook Band of Micmacs,** based in Presque Isle, Maine, is a federally recognized tribe with land holdings throughout the state. Website features include tribal history, traditional culture, an annual festival, and a Powwow or *Mawiomi.*
See: https://micmac-nsn.gov

The **Nulhegan Band of the Coosuk Abenaki Nation** at Nulhegan-Memphremagog, based in Barton, Vermont: a state recognized tribe featuring efforts to preserve the culture, natural resources, and language ("Western Abenaki") through videos, personal stories, a historical timeline, and more.
See: https://abenakitribe.org

Southern New England
The **Wampanoags, "People of the Light." The Mashpee-Wampanoag Tribe:** The Mashpees in Barnstable County, MA, one of three surviving tribes of the original sixty-nine in the Wampanoag Nation. Website features include historical and cultural timelines, contemporary events, and issues. https://mashpeewampanoagtribe-nsn.gov
See also: Wampanoag Tribe of Aquinnah, Martha's Vineyard, MA.
See https://wampanoagtribe-nsn.gov
See also the exhibit: **"Our" Story: 400 Years of Wampanoag History** at the Plymouth 400 Commemoration.
See: https://www.plymouth400inc.org

The Narragansett Indian Nation of Rhode Island: official website of the **"People from the Small Point"** or similar rendition (suggesting Point Judith today). Website features include early history and contemporary concerns.
See: https://narragansettindiannation.org

The Podunks or Pautunke, "The People living in the Place between the Rivers." Excerpts of writings by historian Mathias Spiess about the Podunks, including the tribe's conflict with the (Algonquin) Pequot-Mohegans. Reprinted in the *Quinnehtukqut Nipmuc News*, vol six, No. 1, Jan. 1999.
See: https://www.nativetech.org/Nipmuc/news/historicalsketch.html

Virginia

The **Powhatan Confederacy** had eight tribes, one of which was the **Mattaponi Nation**. See: https://www.mattaponination.com. Also: The Jamestown-Yorktown Foundation offers a Learning Center about the Jamestown Settlement and the American Revolution. Concerning Pocahontas and the Powhatan contact with the English, find essays entitled "Who Were the Powhatan Indians and How Did They Live?" and "What Happened to the Powhatan Culture by the End of the 17th Century?" Look for website menu items "Learn," then "Research and Collections," and then "Essays."
See: https://jfymuseums.org
A National Park Service link about "Historic Jamestowne" features a chronology called "Powhatan Indian Activity" from pre-1607 to 2011.
See: https://www.nps.gov/jame/learn/historyculture/chronology-of-powhatan-indian-activity.htm

Cultural Centers and Museums

Our Story Bridge: Preserving the oral histories of communities small and large is the mission of www.ourstorybridge.org, a national charitable non-profit organization. It supports the creation of locally produced short audio stories and online postings. The Igiugig Tribe was the first Native Alaskan community to record its history in a project called the "Igiugig Story Bridge." Two other Alaskan tribes and a school district are now doing the same.

National Maritime Museum, London, UK, part of Royal Museums Greenwich. Look for "The History of Britain at Sea."
See: https://www.rmg.co.uk

National Maritime Museum, (*Het Scheepvaartmuseum*) Amsterdam, NL. An "Interactive Museum in former storehouse with virtual voyages & replica, 18th-century merchant ship." The museum acknowledges and regrets the country's historic role in the slave trade.
See: https://www.hetscheepvaartmuseum.nl

Westfries Museum in Hoorn, NL. Regional history of the Hoorn seaport in NL.
See: www.westfriesmuseum.info

Connecticut River Museum, Essex, CT, USA. Art & artifacts relating to the area's shipbuilding history (from 1733 onward), plus model ships.
See: https://ctrivermuseum.org

The New Amsterdam History Center, New York, NY, USA features a virtual re-creation of the colonial Dutch settlement and its inhabitants based on archival documents, including the Castello map of 1660.
See: https://newamsterdamhistorycenter.org

The New Netherland Institute, Albany, NY, USA. features the history and culture of New Netherland and offers resources for students and teachers. The *Tour of New Netherland* features details about specific Dutch colonies from Connecticut to Delaware.
See: https://www.newnetherlandinstitute.org

The Institute for American Indian Studies (Museum and Research Center), Washington, Connecticut, USA. It features archeological artifacts of Connecticut's Indigenous peoples, educational programs, virtual learning, summer camps, a "Wigwam Escape" experience for young people, and much more. Also: Teacher Resources with a list of Indigenous authors.
See: https://www.iaismuseum.org

National Museum of the American Indian, New York, NY, USA. "Native American art & artifacts, some going back 12,000 years, displayed in a former customs house." Efforts are now being made nationally to return sacred artifacts, especially funerary objects and human remains, to their proper (Native) owners.
See: http://nmai.si.edu

The New York State Museum, Albany, NY, USA. Among its exhibits: 1.) *The Prehistoric Wilderness Landscape*, featuring some of the animals that inhabited the Adirondacks during the events of

The River Quintet, and 2.) three dioramas of a Mohawk-Iroquois village ca. 1600.
See: https://www.nysm.nysed.gov.

The **Iroquois Indian Museum,** located in Howes Cave, NY. Modeled after an Iroquois longhouse, the museum exposes visitors to Iroquois culture through storytelling, nature walks, and contemporary arts and crafts.
See: https://www.iroquoismuseum.org

Student Resources

Native American Facts for Kids. List of Native Indian Tribes and Languages.
See: http://www.native-languages.org/languages.htm

Kidinfo: Native Americans: Histories and Facts.
See: https://www. kidinfo.com/american history/native americans. html

Indian Country Today: a multi-digital platform with sections devoted to news, newscasts, classifieds, opinion, culture, arts, and entertainment relating to Indigenous tribes "throughout the Americas" and "outside" news of U.S. and international importance.
See: https://indiancountrytoday.com

"6 Nations of the Iroquois Confederacy": short and simple pictorial overview of the Iroquois Confederacy by Jeff Wallenfeldt.

See: https://www.britannica.com/list-the-6-nations-of-the-iroquois-confederacy

American History Tellers: "Dutch Manhattan," podcast episodes by Wondery.
See: https://www.wondery.com/shows/american-history-tellers/season15

An Introduction to Stuart England (1603-1714): On the main site (English Heritage) choose "Learn," then "Story of England," then "Stuarts." The pictorial overview will open.
See: https://www.english-heritage.org.uk

The New England Colonies: overview of the religious groups that settled the Massachusetts Bay and Plymouth Colonies; just one of many websites on this subject.
See: https://www.ushistory.org/us/3.asp

Deafness: YouTube videos: "Understanding Deafness-Educational Video," Jessica Le, 2012; "Kids Meet a Deaf Person," Hiho Kids, 2017; and "Through the Eyes of Deaf Children," *The Atlantic,* 2018, and more! Also: PBS Nova educational documentary: "The Mystery of the Senses," episode: Hearing.

The Limping Chicken Blog: news, stories, advice, book and film reviews and much more for the deaf and hearing-impaired global community.
See: https//limpingchicken.com

Suggested Reading

For Younger Students — Middle School
Bruchac, Joseph. *Hidden Roots.* New York: Scholastic Books, 2004. About an Abenaki boy. (The author, a reteller of Native American folktales, is of Abenaki heritage.)

Robertson Robbie, author and David Shannon, illustrator. *Hiawatha and The Peacemaker.* New York: Abrams Books for Young people, 2015. (The author is of Mohawk and Cayuga heritage.)

Townsend, Camilla and Nicky Kay Michael. *On the Turtle's Back: Stories the Lenapes Told Their Grandchildren.* New Brunswick, NJ: Rutgers University Press, 2023.

For a list of Indigenous authors see 1). "Teacher Resources" of The Institute for American Indian Studies cited under Museums and Cultural Centers, and 2. the next book by Dunbar-Ortiz, pp. 231-234.

For Older Students — High School
Dunbar-Ortiz, Roxanne. *The Indigenous Peoples' History of the United States – Adapted for Young People.* Boston: Beacon Press, 2014. Adapted by Jean Mendoza and Debbie Reese. Provides a critical view of U. S. history in terms of its treatment of Indigenous populations. http://www.beacon.org

For Adults

Jacobs, Jaap. *The Colony of New Netherland: A Dutch Settlement in the Seventeenth Century*. Ithaca: Cornell University Press, 2009.
See also: https://www.cornellpress.edu

Rountree, Helen C.: *Pocahontas, Powhatan, Opechancanough: Three Indian Lives Changed by Jamestown*. Charlottesville: University of Virginia Press, 2006.
See: https://www.upress.virginia.edu

Shorto, Russell. *The Island at the Center of the World: The Epic Story of Dutch Manhattan and the Forgotten Colony That Shaped America*. New York: Vintage Books, 2005.
See: https://www.russellshorto.com

Soderlund, Jean. *Lenape Country: Delaware Valley Society Before William Penn* (Early American Studies). Philadelphia, PA: University of Pennsylvania Press, 2016.

Starna, William A., and C.T. Gehring, eds.: *A Description of New Netherland* by Adriaen van der Donck translated by Diederik Willem Goedhuys. Lincoln: University of, Nebraska Press, 2008.

Strobel, Christoph. *Native Americans of New England*. Westport, CT: Prager Publishers, 2020.
See: https://www.amazon.com

Winship, Michael P. *Hot Protestants: A History of Puritanism in England and America*. New Haven: Yale University Press, 2019.
See: https://www.amazon.com

9 798989 906307